A-LEVEL YEAR 2 PSYCHOLOGY FOR EDEXCEL

UNIT 2C (Applications: Child Psychology)

CHILD PSYCHOLOGY STUDY GUIDE

Published independently by Tinderspark Press
© Jonathan Rowe 2018
www.psychologywizard.net

CONTENTS

ABOUT THIS BOOK

This book offers advice for teachers and students approaching Edexcel A-Level Psychology, Paper 2 (Applications), Topic C (Child Psychology). There are two other "applications" to choose from:

B   Criminological Psychology

D   Health Psychology

To be clear, candidates only need to answer on ONE of these applications in the exam. There is no expectation that candidates prepare for two or all three of these applications and in fact this is NOT recommended.

Candidates will also need to prepare for the compulsory application:

A   Clinical Psychology

Material for Clinical Psychology can be found freely available on the **www.psychologywizard.net** website along with material for Paper 1 (Foundations).

Study Guides for Paper 3 (Issues & Debates) will follow.

Text that is indented and shaded like this is a quotation from a researcher or participant. Candidates could use some of these quotations in their exam responses but this is not mandatory.

Text in this typeface and boxed represents the author's comments, observations and reflections. Such texts are not intended to guide candidates in writing exam answers (i.e. don't go quoting ME!)

TOPIC 2C: CHILD PSYCHOLOGY

Child Psychology is the study of the mental, social and emotional development of children from birth through to adolescence. As well as changes in motor skills (movement), it focuses on cognitive development (thinking), language acquisition and how we form our identity.

Childhood is a time of rapid growth and development. Studying these changes also tells us a about adult behaviour. In this course, you will be introduced to some of the key questions about childhood: *'What influences children's development?'* and *'How do psychologists study the physical and cognitive changes that occur during childhood?'* Crucial to answering these questions are DEVELOPMENTAL MILESTONES – changes in thinking and behaviour that happen to ALL healthy humans in the same order and at similar times.

A key issue in Child Psychology is the NATURE/NURTURE DEBATE (pp52, 72, 107): are children born with abilities or is everything learned from the early environment? This is SOCIALLY SENSITIVE (p110), because conclusions about childcare influence parenting and teaching as well as working arrangements and the role of women in society.

- **Parents** want to know how best to raise their children. Is it a good idea to let your children cope without you or should you keep them close? Do they have a special bond with their mothers or can fathers be carers instead?
- **Teachers** want to know how to stimulate children and help them develop their cognitive and social skills. Are there appropriate ages for learning certain skills or can they be learned at any time? Do all children develop at the same rate? What should be done with developmental disorders in children?

Working arrangements are a **socially sensitive** topic. Early child psychologists like **John Bowlby** suggested that, by leaving the home to work, mothers were damaging their children emotionally. Other researchers have claimed that putting children into **daycare** actually improves children's skills rather than setting them back. This debate has a big impact on **women**, who will have more equality in society if they work or study, but who may experience pressure to be stay-at-home mothers instead.

> *Remember that the title of this unit is "Applications of Psychology" so you should make a point of relating research to these issues: how might teachers, parents and working mums respond to these psychological ideas?*

The DAYCARE DEBATE is the main issue raised by this application of Psychology: should we be putting our children into daycare to allow both parents to work or study? or would it be better for children to be cared for at home by their own parents, even if this holds back women in particular from fulfilling their other ambitions?

CHILD PSYCHOLOGY: CONTENT

What's this topic about?

This introduces you to the main theories in Child Psychology, in particular the concept of ATTACHMENT (p7) and what happens when attachment fails to occur, due to PRIVATION (p14), DEPRIVATION (p19) or a developmental disorder like AUTISM (p43). You will also learn about cultural variations in attachment (such as different parenting styles in different parts of the world), developmental differences (such as how attachment changes at different ages) and individual differences (such as how all this links to the child's personality). You will have covered some of these ideas already as part of the AS or Year 1 course:

Social Psychology

Milgram suggests that children are socialised into recognizing and obeying authority figures by their parents. The cultural variations in obedience (e.g. the 1974 **Kilham & Mann** variation in Australia) suggest that parents from different cultures raise children with different responses to authority – some are very obedient, others (like the Australians) find it easy to rebel. **Adorno**'s concept of the AUTHORITARIAN PERSONALITY is also based on the idea that some people are influenced for the rest of their lives by their strict and un-loving parents.

Cognitive Psychology

Memory seems to be a CULTURAL UNIVERSAL – something that works the same for all humans regardless of their background or upbringing. However, **Nelson** (2004) reports that Asians tend to have earlier childhood memories than Europeans and Americans. She thinks this is because Asian parents start talking to their children about their memories at a younger age.

Biological Psychology

Raine's study of brain deficits in murderers leaves the question of whether the murderers were born with these deficits (nature) or whether they acquired them because of the sort of experiences they had as children (nurture). In this topic, you will find out about **Bowlby**'s warning that depriving children of their mothers turns them into *"affectionless psychopaths."* **Freud**'s theory about the development of the unconscious mind is very important for Child Psychology.

Learning Theories

Behaviourists (psychologists like **Watson** and **Skinner**) argue that childhood development is based on STIMULUS AND RESPONSE. John Watson famously claimed that if he was given *"a dozen healthy infants"* he could raise them to be anything he wanted using conditioning techniques, regardless of the child's abilities and (significantly for America in the 1930s) the child's race. **Bandura** in the 1960s went on to show how children develop through observation and imitation.

ATTACHMENT

Attachment is the bond between an animal and its parent – usually its mother. It is vital in learning and in social development and it seems to have effects which carry on into adult life. Attachment is observed in all animals.

The term "attachment" was coined by British psychologist **John Bowlby** who defined it as:

the lasting psychological connectedness between human beings **– John Bowlby**

Bowlby's work was co-developed by **Mary Ainsworth**:

Attachment is a deep and enduring emotional bond that connects one person to another across time and space **– Mary Ainsworth**

But what *causes* this process of attachment?

THE EVOLUTIONARY BASIS FOR ATTACHMENT

*In **Unit 1**, you studied **evolution** as part of the **Biological Approach**, as an explanation of **aggression**. You should revise it now as an explanation of attachment.*

Charles Darwin's Theory of Evolution proposes that humans have evolved from ape-like ancestors and will therefore develop in ways similar to other animals.

Attachment may be a **survival trait** – something that makes a creature more likely to survive and grow up to reproduce. Animals that have genes that favour attachment have an advantage over animals that don't – they are more likely to be cared for and protected by their parents. They are also more likely to suffer psychologically and physically without their parent's presence, but overall there are more advantages than disadvantages to attachment.

Genes that encourage survival traits become more common within a population over time. Today, all humans (and other animals) are descended from ancestors that have these genes which is why we all experience attachment.

This is the view that attachment is a biological process: it is NATURE rather than NURTURE (pp52, 72, 107), a sort of instinct that we have no control over.

The study of behaviour from an evolutionary viewpoint is **ETHOLOGY** and one of the most famous ethologists to study attachment is **Karl Lorenz**. Lorenz noticed that ducks and geese, when hatched, follow the first moving object they see; this is called IMPRINTING.

Usually, ducklings imprint on their mother, but occasionally they can imprint on another animal or a human, with comical results.

Human infants don't "imprint" on a mother as immediately and as dramatically as ducklings, but something similar does go on in a subtle way. **John Bowlby** combined this insight from ethology with Freud's insight from psychodynamic theory to create his own MATERNAL DEPRIVATION HYPOTHESIS.

ROBERTSON'S "A TWO-YEAR-OLD GOES TO HOSPITAL"

James Robertson was a research colleague of Bowlby's who had also worked with Freud's daughter, **Anna Freud**. Robertson studied children at Anna Freud's children's hospital and noticed the distress they showed when they were separated from their mothers. He made a 1953 film about a 2-year-old girl called Laura who was in hospital for 8 days for an operation. The film put forward the view (which wasn't widely accepted at the time) that children suffered when their attachment figure wasn't near.

WHAT?!? Did people in the early 20th century really not notice that their children got upset when they were apart? Remember that the middle and upper classes routinely employed nannies or sent their children to boarding schools (Bowlby went to a boarding school and hated it), so the idea that this might be bad for children was slow to take hold

Robertson's study of Laura was a **case study** and a **naturalistic observation** (p60). He kept the procedure scientific by sampling the girl's behaviour at random intervals over 8 days. He observed 3 stages in the loss of attachment

1. **Protest:** the child cries and throws tantrums, showing anger and fear
2. **Despair:** crying becomes intermittent and the child seems to be settling down, but distress is really deepening
3. **Detachment:** the child seems content but really the attachment is breaking and long-term emotional damage may take place

This is the PDD (PROTEST–DESPAIR–DETACHMENT) MODEL of separation.

HARLOW'S MONKEYS

Harry Harlow (1958) is notorious in the history of Psychology for his experiments on rhesus monkeys to explore attachment.

These infant monkeys were taken away from their mothers and encouraged to become attached to two objects known as SURROGATES (replacements):

Wire mother [*left*] and cloth mother [*right*]

- WIRE MOTHER: a metal frame that provides milk through a teat
- CLOTH MOTHER: no milk but wrapped in a soft terry cloth that provides comfort

Harlow observed that monkeys that had access to both surrogates developed into healthier adults than those who only had access to a wire surrogate. This shows that attachment is not just about food (which the wire mother provided), but emotional comfort as well.

When Harlow used loud noises and lights to frighten the monkeys, those with access to a cloth mother would run to 'her' for comfort then show courage; those with no cloth mother would simply cower.

*Harlow's experiments revealed a great deal about attachment but were condemned for the **unethical treatment of animals** - which verged on the sadistic.*

John Bowlby was inspired by Harlow's ideas (but not his methods) and concluded that the **protest stage** of the PDD (when infants are separated from their attachment figure) might also be a **survival trait** – the loud protest attracts the attention of the caregiver and (hopefully) brings her back. This is called a SOCIAL RELEASER because by crying the baby triggers social behaviour in the caregiver (to come and pay attention).

FREUD'S PSYCHODYNAMIC PERSPECTIVE

> *In Unit 1, you studied **Freud's psychodynamic theory** of **aggression**. It would be good to revise that while learning psychodynamic ideas of attachment.*

Sigmund Freud was one of the first psychologists to consider attachment in humans as an explanation of lifelong behaviours. Freud's psychodynamic theory proposes that our personality forms through our childhood relationship with our parents.

- In the first months of life, we develop an **id** – the instinct for pleasure and survival
- In the second year of life, the **ego** develops – the self-aware part of the mind that can understand reality
- Around the fifth year of life, the **super-ego** forms – this is the moral part of the mind that experiences guilt and shame

The super-ego is particularly linked to our parents. Freud argues that we internalise the values of our same-sex parents (girls' mothers, boys' fathers) but that this process is difficult and full of conflict – he calls it the "OEDIPUS COMPLEX".

- An **under-developed super-ego** can leave us without clear moral values: without a strong sense of shame, we can be selfish and dishonest
- An **over-developed super-ego** can leave us with incredibly strict values, but tormented by feelings of shame and worthlessness: haunted by a need for punishment, we misbehave to attract attention from powerful people

Many psychologists were impressed by Freud's focus on early childhood as the source of later problems, but found his ideas of an Oedipus Complex too UNSCIENTIFIC (p109). **John Bowlby** adopted Freud's focus on child-parent relationships but adopted a more scientific and measurable approach.

SPITZ'S INSTITUTIONALISED CHILDREN

René Spitz (1946) studied children in hospitals and identified that they became **depressed** when away from their attachment figure.

Spitz concluded that if an infant forms an attachment with the mother in the first 6 months of life, the child will develop in a healthy way. If the attachment is broken (such as by a stay in hospital) then the child suffers ANACLITIC DEPRESSION – the infant wastes away emotionally, socially and physically and can even die.

Short breaks in attachment can be recovered from; if the child is reunited with its mother it re-attaches in a couple of months.

However, longer detachment can become severe and Spitz terms this HOSPITALISM. Three months seems to be the crucial period: before that time, the child will try to form attachments with nurses and carers and cling to them, but after that the child becomes severely depressed and withdraws. These hospitalised children lose weight and stop showing facial expression; they refuse to interact with carers or playmates.

Spitz didn't just blame hospitalism on separation from the attachment figure. He also blamed lack of stimulation in hospitals where there was nothing for the child to look at or play with. He linked this to institutionalised children having low IQs.

In 1990, after the fall of Romania's Communist regime, thousands of orphans were discovered living neglected in state orphanages in shocking conditions. The mental states of these Romanian orphans resembled Spitz's description of hospitalism (**Rutter *et al.*, 2007**). Many Romanian orphans were adopted by families in Europe and America and these INTERNATIONAL ADOPTEES (IAs) taught psychologists a lot about attachment.

EVALUATING THEORIES OF ATTACHMENT AO3

Credibility

The research by Robertson and by Spitz used **naturalistic observation** – real children in real hospitals – carried out with **standardised procedures** that reduced researcher effects.

Robertson's film can be watched today and his conclusions checked. Robertson replicated his procedure with later observations of other children undergoing **short term separation and deprivation** and he observed the same responses (distress, despair, detachment).

Spitz also replicated his research on other children and carried out **longitudinal research**, measuring changes to children's IQ scores over time, which supports his hypothesis that **long term separation and deprivation** is particularly harmful, especially when there is a lack of stimulation as well as attachment.

Harlow's research was also **standardized and objective** (so much so that it appears particularly callous and cruel today). The fearful reactions of the rhesus monkeys clinging to the cloth mother for comfort have **face validity** (it's clear that the monkeys are frightened). Rhesus monkeys share 93% of their genes with humans, which justifies **generalising** from infant monkeys to infant humans, to some extent.

Schaffer & Emerson (1964) found that human babies form attachments to other people beside their mother (like the father, uncles, big sisters) – this backs up Harlow's conclusion that attachment isn't just about a source of food.

Objections

Naturalistic observations in hospitals suffer problems of reliability, because the children will be affected by other people (visitors, the behaviour of nurses and doctors) as well as the situation itself (like being sick and undergoing an operation). There's even a tendency for the children to form attachments to the researchers. This weakens the conclusions that can be drawn from Robertson's and Spitz's research into attachment.

Spitz's research suffers from particular problems because it is hard to measure IQ reliably in very young children. Unlike Robertson, Spitz didn't use careful sampling and controls; he focused on children who already seemed to be suffering problems in hospital (rather than a representative sample of all the children in hospital) and he based his measures of distress and IQ on personal observations and interviews rather than anything objective. This means Spitz's research may reflect his own beliefs and prejudices rather than attachment.

In fact, Spitz and Robertson and a lot of researchers from this era carried out research that was highly SUBJECTIVE (personal opinion) without much in the way of standardised procedures. The work of **Mary Ainsworth** (p33) in the 1960s and '70s would change this.

Harlow's research lacked ecological validity because he kept the rhesus monkeys in strange and unnatural conditions – nothing about their life and experience was 'normal' for a monkey. Some of his test monkeys were the offspring of earlier test monkeys, so Harlow's lab was all they had ever known.

Despite the 93% similarity in genes, humans and rhesus monkeys differ in 7% of their genome and this might include important genes for development and attachment. Generalising from rhesus monkeys to human infants might not be meaningful.

> *Of course, Harlow's research was horribly unethical too - but be careful about raising this because the poor ethics of a piece of research doesn't damage its SCIENTIFIC conclusions. Harlow might be right (scientifically) about attachment even though he was wrong (ethically) for treating the monkeys this way.*

Differences

The psychodynamic and evolutionary explanations of attachment can be contrasted.

Both theories are different from the previously-accepted behavioural theory of attachment (**Dollard & Miller, 1950**), which downplayed the child's bond with their mother. The behavioural theory of attachment stated that the child learns to be attached to the mother because she feeds the infant– therefore, anyone who feeds the infants fulfils its needs for attachment (also known as the CUPBOARD LOVE THEORY).

The psychodynamic explanations focus on human emotions and assume that infants have essentially the same emotions as adults, possibly even more intense, but that they express those emotions differently because of their lack of language or social skills.

These explanations are "human-centred" and reject animal studies as unrepresentative. They focus strongly on the mother-child relationship, suggesting that the mother provides emotional comfort for the infant that other caregivers (like fathers) cannot.

Evolutionary explanations focus on behaviour rather than emotion. They identify attachment as a behaviour that has survival value and comes from genes. These explanations are not "human-centred" because they apply to *all* living creatures. As a result, animal studies can tell us a lot about attachment in humans. They suggest that "surrogates" can provide some of what the infant needs (so, for example, a father could be the caregiver for an infant just as well as a mother), however the infant needs more than just food from a caregiver, but also a sense of security.

John Bowlby combined both explanations in his MATERNAL DEPRIVATION HYPOTHESIS (p19).

Applications

Robertson's film led to changes in how hospitals treat sick children. In the 1950s, hospital visiting times usually involved just two hours on a Sunday – some hospitals (such as St Thomas's, London) didn't allow any visitors at all for the first month (but parents could come in and watch their baby sleeping).

In NHS hospitals today, there are usually open visiting hours every day and parents can stay overnight, sleeping beside the child in a reclining chair. This is a direct application of Robertson's research. Hospitals usually provide a play room for children and trained play assistants to make sure they are stimulated. This is an application of **Spitz**'s research.

PRIVATION

Research into **attachment** shows that, without an attachment figure, infants do not develop in a healthy way. However, a lot of this research ignores *why* the attachment is missing. **Michael Rutter (1972)** wrote *Maternal Deprivation Re-assessed* and distinguished between **privation** and **deprivation**. Rutter argues that

- **deprivation** (p19) is when attachment forms but is later lost or damaged, but
- **privation** is when a child fails to develop an attachment in the first place

Privation occurs when there is a failure to form an attachment to a single individual – the primary caregiver. This might happen because:

- the child has a series of different carers (which was the case for many of **Bowlby**'s juvenile thieves, *c.f.* p25)
- family disruption prevents attachment to any single figure (as Rutter proposed)
- abuse or neglect means the child receives no attention from anyone (as is the case with feral children and with Genie, below)

Privated children do not show distress when separated from a familiar figure; this is the evidence for their lack of attachment.

In the long term, privated children show clinging behaviour at first: they are attention-seeking and indiscriminate in their friendliness (accepting affection from anyone, even strangers). As the child matures, they are unable to keep rules, form lasting relationships or feel guilt.

> *The lack of guilt links to **Bowlby's** "affectionless psychopathy" as well as **Freud's** underdeveloped super-ego*

Michael Rutter (1976) carried out a survey on the Isle of Wight, involving interviews with 2000 boys, aged 9-12, and their families. The boys were 4 times more likely to be delinquent if their attachment problems came from family discord (PRIVATION) rather than the illness or death of the mother (DEPRIVATION). Among the privated children, Rutter recorded anti-social behaviour and disorders of language, IQ and physical growth.

Rutter argues that these problems are not entirely due to lack of attachment to a mother figure. Attachments also provide intellectual stimulation and social experiences, which privated children lack. However, Rutter believes these problems can be overcome later in the child's development, with the right kind of care

EXAMPLES OF PRIVATION

A FERAL CHILD is a child who has been isolated from human contact, interfering with their development of human social skills. Feral children miss out on the most basic socialization. This leads some psychologists suggest that there is a CRITICAL PERIOD for attachment. After this point, the child cannot be properly socialized into normal human behaviour

The most popular idea of a feral child involves a child raised in the woods by animals. This is a common idea in fiction and it has occurred in reality. However, children do not have to live in nature to become feral. Extreme abuse and neglect can also interfere with normal development.

Feral children tend to take on the characteristics of their environment: a child raised in the woods might be more comfortable around animals, but a child abandoned in a basement might be afraid to leave enclosed spaces.

Feral children have been reported throughout history. The most famous was **Victor of Aveyron (1797)**, who was found living wild in the woods at the age of 12. Victor was unable to speak and never learned human language, despite the lifelong efforts of a French doctor to teach him.

Der Wilde von Aveyron.

RAISED BY DOGS: OXANA MALAYA

In 1991, Oxana Malaya was found in the Ukraine; she was 8 and had lived among wild dogs since the age of 3 when her alcoholic parents had abandoned her. She showed dog-like behaviour such as barking, walking on all fours, sniffing and digging and eating raw meat. She had formed a powerful bond with the dogs; when the authorities tried to rescue her, the dogs protected her. The only words she could speak were 'yes' and 'no'.

After being rescued, Oxana found it difficult to learn normal language and behaviour. However, therapy in a home for mentally disabled children helped her overcome these difficulties to varying degrees. Oxana is not 'normal' and is unlikely to live a life without care, but she now speaks, walks and eats normally and has relationships.

> *It's not clear whether Oxana's recovery was due to successful care, the advantage of spending the first 3 years with her parents or the social interaction she experienced with the dogs. Oxana works on a farm now and cares for animals. She wants a human life and does not wish to be known as "the Dog Girl". I hope students respect that when referring to Oxana in the Exam.*

LOCKED IN THE CELLAR: THE CZECH TWINS

Andrei and Vanya are identical twin boys who lost their mother shortly after they were born in 1960 in Czechoslovakia . They were orphaned in the first year of life but then returned to live with their father. However, their new step-mother made them live in the cellar for the next 5½ years, beating them on occasions.

When they were rescued at the age of 7, the twins were very small in stature; they lacked speech and did not understand the meaning of pictures. The doctors who examined them predicted they would suffer permanent physical and mental disability. The twins first went on a physical health programme and were put into a school for children with severe learning disabilities. Later, the boys were adopted by an dedicated carer. The twins caught up with their school peers and developed into emotionally and intellectual normal children, according to the **case study** by **Jarmila Koluchová (1972)**.

The twins later went to college, married and had children. They are said to be entirely stable and in warm relationships, according to **Clarke & Clarke (1998)**. One is a computer technician and the other a technical training instructor.

> *The Czech Twins are uplifting examples of the effects of privation being reversed. However, they had each other for companionship, which makes them unlike Oxana (above) or Genie (below).*

THE CASE OF GENIE

Susan Curtiss (1977) describes one of the most famous (and tragic) cases of extreme privation.

Genie Wiley was born in California in 1957. Genie's father believed she was mentally disabled so, when she was 20 months of age and was just beginning to learn speech, he locked his daughter in a room, isolated from the rest of the family.

Genie spent the next 12 years of her life locked in her bedroom. During the day, she was tied to a child's potty chair in diapers; at night, she was tied up in a sleeping bag and placed in a box. Genie's father beat her if she spoke and he growled at her like a dog to keep her quiet. He prevented his wife and son from interacting with Genie.

Genie was rescued at the age of 13 when her mother left her husband. Genie could not stand upright and scored as low as a normal 1-year-old for social maturity. She could only understand her own name, didn't know how to chew and was not toilet trained.

Genie was sent to live with the family of a research scientist who studied her language development while trying to socialize her and care for her. She advanced to one-word answers and learned to dress herself. Her intelligence advanced to that of a 5-year-old.

However, Genie didn't progress the way normal children would do: she never asked questions, did not understand grammar and her vocabulary did not increase beyond 30 words, although she did learn to express herself through sign language. She had fits of rage but never cried

Towards the end of the study, Genie (now 18) had begun to talk about her father (who had committed suicide) and (it seems) recall her abuse:

> *Father hit big stick. Father is angry. Father hit Genie big stick. Father take piece wood hit. Cry. Father make me cry. Father is dead* – **Genie**

Genie's therapy was cut short. The study lost its funding and Genie was returned to her mother. However, Genie's mother was unable to cope with her and give her up to a string of 6 foster homes. Genie suffered isolation and abuse in these homes and she regressed (moved backwards) in her behaviour. Genie stopped speaking altogether.

Genie never reached normal cognitive or emotional development. She now lives in a sheltered accommodation in California, with her anonymity preserved. Her mother died in 2003 but Genie has never spoken again.

> *Genie's story is tragic, because the researchers trying to treat her failed to help her and her privation was not reversed. A string of mistakes, legal disputes, personality clashes and petty disagreements led to Genie becoming "lost in the system".*

EVALUATING THEORIES OF PRIVATION AO3

Credibility

Rutter's theory is that privation is a different condition from **deprivation**: it is more destructive and harder to reverse. There is evidence to support this from Rutter's 'Isle of Wight' study, which showed greater social and emotional problems among the privated boys. Rutter's research had a very large sample. The concept of privation is also supported by the condition of feral children, who seem to experience exceptional problems learning basic social skills, language and intellectual development.

Curtiss' case study of Genie suggests that privated children may never develop fully in language, intelligence and social behaviour, compared to children who have normal attachments or deprived children who receive care and therapy later in life.

Objections

Research into feral children is often anecdotal (story-based) or retrospective (after the fact). It's often not possible to study feral children from the moment of their discovery through to adulthood. It's hard to know how 'normal' the children were to begin with.

- Oxana Malaya *seemed* normal as an infant, but her parents were alcoholics
- The Czech twins *seemed* normal, but their father had learning difficulties
- Genie Wiley was diagnosed by a family doctor as mentally sub-normal at the age of 1, which encouraged her unstable father to regard her as retarded

Curtiss' case study of Genie is one of the few opportunities to study a feral child closely and scientifically, but this seems to have caused problems too: Genie's mother alleged that excessive testing had damaged Genie's development

It's not even clear whether these cases are true examples of privation, since all of these children had (relatively) normal upbringing for the first year of life. Oxana and Genie both began to speak before they were shut away. If there are no definite cases of privation to study, privation is just an extreme form of deprivation rather than a separate condition.

Differences

Rutter criticises **Bowlby's** theory of MATERNAL DEPRIVATION. Many of the "44 thieves" in Bowlby's study (p25) had moved around a lot during childhood and had probably never formed an attachment. This suggests that they were suffering from privation, rather than deprivation, which Rutter claims is far more damaging to the children.

Applications

It is not clear whether the effects of privation can be fully reversed. Rutter was hopeful that care and therapy could reverse privation. This is supported by the case study of the **Czech twins** (who made a full recovery) and **Oxana Malaya** (who made a partial but significant recovery).

However, evidence also suggests that privation may be irreversible. The Czech twins may not have been privated at all, since they had each other as companions. Oxana Malaya is happy but does not live independently and is not socially normal. **Genie Wiley** showed some progress but completely regressed after the case study ended; even during the study, her progress was far slower than was hoped for.

Most psychologists conclude there is a CRITICAL PERIOD in early childhood (before age 5, **Bowby** argues the first 18 months) when attachments form successfully. If this doesn't happen, children find it hard to form attachments later on.

DEPRIVATION

The pioneering research into **attachment** was carried out by British psychologist **John Bowlby**. Bowlby coined the word "attachment" and combined Freudian and evolutionary ideas into his theory of MATERNAL DEPRIVATION.

Bowlby argues that, while growing up, it is essential that a child enjoys

> *a warm, intimate and continuous relationship with a mother* – **John Bowlby**

He also claims that

> *Mother-love in infancy is as important for mental health as are vitamins and proteins for physical health* – **John Bowlby**

Bowlby proposes that separation from the mother is deeply traumatic for the growing child and causes last psychological damage.

MATERNAL DEPRIVATION THEORY

John Bowlby suggests that the most important attachment figure in a child's life is the mother. Children who are deprived of the mother's comforting presence experience psychological problems.

Bowlby was inspired by **Karl Lorenz** and the **ethological** approach to human behaviour (based on the **Theory of Evolution**, *c.f.* p7). Lorenz showed that attachment was innate (in young ducklings) and therefore has a survival value.

Bowlby (1969) concludes that attachment in humans is also instinctive; he also suggests that the fear of strangers is another SURVIVAL TRAIT.

Bowlby concludes that both infants and mothers have evolved a biological need to stay in contact with each other. Babies are born with certain innate behaviours (SOCIAL RELEASERS) which help keep close contact with the mother or attachment figure (eg. crying, smiling). During the evolution of humans, babies who stayed close to their mothers (or encouraged their mothers to stay close to them) would have survived to have children of their own. The infant's 'social releasers' such as crying and smiling produce caregiving from adults. The basis of attachment is not food but care and responsiveness.

> *Bowlby's focus in innate behaviour was a move away from the behavioural theory of attachment, which claimed that all the infant's behaviours are learned and that food was the basis of attachment. You studied the importance of learning in babies with the **Unit 1 study by Watson & Rayner about Baby Albert**.*

Bowlby suggests that a child initially forms **only one attachment** – this is called MONOTROPY. The attachment figure acts as a safe haven (a secure base) for exploring the world. At first, Bowlby argued the monotropic bond could only be with the mother.

> *Remember **Harlow's monkeys**? The monkeys with a cloth mother showed courage when faced with a frightening object or an unfamiliar environment: the surrogate mother acted as a safe haven for them.*

However, Bowlby also draws on the **psychodynamic view of attachment** (p10) because he suggests that the monotropic bond acts as a template for all future relationships. If monotropic attachment is secure, the child will grow up to find other intimate, trusting relationships easy; if attachment is disrupted, future relationships will have problems too. These problems include delinquency in teenage years and AFFECTIONLESS PSYCHOPATHY (no concern for others).

The psychodynamic psychologist **Melanie Klein** suggests **object relations theory**: this is the idea that children construct fantasy relationships (with parents but also with dolls and toys) that are the basis for all their future relationships. They form an INTERNAL WORKING MODEL for how all future relationships should be.

> *Does this "internal working model" sound like a set of **schemas** to you? Now would be a good time to revise **Bartlett's schema theory of memory** from Unit 1.*

Bowlby adapts the ideas of object relations theory. He thinks children do create these internal working models, but based on the real relationship with their attachment figure, rather than fantasy relationships. If the monotropic bond is broken, the infant constructs a destructive internal working model based on anger, fear and distrust.

Bowlby suggests that, for the infant, being deprived of their attachment figure is a loss rather like the death of a loved one for an adult: the infant goes through grief. Bowlby argues that mother and child should not separate for the first 18 months of the childs life and should only be apart for short periods for the first 3-4 years.

Anne Tracey (2011) interviewed 26 women whose mothers had died in childhood. They were more likely to be depressed as adults and recalled yearning for a mother figure during their childhood and adolescence. The absence of a mother

undermined their self-esteem and sense of security – **Anne Tracey**

The women in Tracey's study talked explicitly about "loss" which backs up Bowlby's conclusions about maternal deprivation being like grief and its effects lasting into adulthood.

SKEELS & DYE: THE IMPORTANCE OF CAREGIVERS

Skeels & Dye (1939) studied 25 1-2 year-old orphans whose IQ was too low for them to be adopted. One group was raised in a normal institution, in which the staff were too busy to give much individual attention.

The other group of 13 were placed in a "*home for feeble-minded women*" and raised by the residents: teenage girls who had learning difficulties (but normal emotional responses).

After 18 months, the average IQ of the children in the orphanage fell from 87 to 61; the children raised by surrogate mothers had a rise in IQ from 64 to 92. This made 11 of the 13 eligible for adoption, whereas all the institutionalised children had to stay in the orphanage.

Skeels & Dye conclude that the emotional care the children received from surrogate mothers in the home reduced the deprivation experienced by the children

Years later, **Howard Skeels (1966)** located all of the participants in the original study.

- Of the 13 children who had been cared for by the young women, 11 had married and had normal healthy children. These participants had achieved a normal level of education: four had attended college.
- Of the 12 children who had remained in the orphanage, four were still institutionalized in 1965; the rest (with one exception) were unskilled labourers with low education.

This suggests the effects of maternal deprivation can last a lifetime but can be reversed by

programs of intervention to counteract the devastating effects of poverty, sociocultural, and maternal deprivation – **Howard Skeels**

EVALUATING THEORIES OF DEPRIVATION AO3

Credibility

Bowlby's theory of maternal deprivation is based on data gathered from a variety of sources: ethological studies like Lorenz and Harlow as well as naturalistic observations in hospitals, such as **Spitz**. He took into account the latest psychodynamic theories (**Anna Freud**, **Melanie Klein**) and the latest evolutionary theories and animal studies. He also organised other research, such as that by James Robertson, and included their findings in this theory.

Bowlby's theory is supported by findings that institutionalisation links with low IQ (**Skeels & Dye**) and with brain dysfunction (**Olsavsky** *et al.*).

Bowlby's theory is also supported by his own study of "44 Juvenile Thieves". **Mary Ainsworth**'s studies using the "Strange Situation" back up the idea of an INTERNAL WORKING MODEL.

Credibility is also boosted by research that shows how a child's brain develops during the critical first 3 years.

Objections

Most of the research supporting Bowlby's theory comes from naturalistic observations in hospitals, orphanages and homes. These studies lack carefully standardised procedures (although the work of **James Robertson** is an exception to this, *c.f.* p8). Many of them selected infants who were already low IQ or emotionally troubled, so it's not clear if deprivation was the true cause of their later problems.

Bowlby's study of **"44 Juvenile Thieves"** (p25) has been criticised, because the control group also included institutionalised children, rather than healthy children without any deprivation.

Animal studies cannot be confidently generalised to humans. Humans differ from animals in possessing language and have superior problem-solving abilities. Human infants develop more slowly than monkeys and form attachments differently.

Skeels (1966) found that the girls who were removed from the orphanage to a caring environment seemed to have completely recovered – they were educationally and emotionally healthy and successful. This suggests maternal deprivation can be reversed. **Michael Rutter** (1972, 1976) has a similar view. This is also backed up by **Schaffer & Emerson (1964**, p54**)**, who found babies could form multiple attachments, which goes against **monotropy** and suggests babies could form an attachment to someone else if deprived of their mother.

The biggest criticism of Bowlby's theory comes from **Michael Rutter**, who points out that Bowlby did not distinguish between **deprivation** (loss of an existing attachment) and **privation** (failure to form an attachment in the first place). Rutter argues that privation is much more serious than deprivation, but that many of Bowlby's cases of damaged children were really privated children, not maternal deprivation at all.

Differences

Bowlby's theory contrasts with the **behavioural theory of attachment**. This theory is based on the **Learning Approach**. It suggests that infants form attachments because they **associate** their caregiver with food (CUPBOARD LOVE). The caregiver is usually the mother, behaviourism argues children form attachments with anyone who feeds them.

This behavioural theory ignores the idea that humans may have **evolved** to form attachments to particular people, rather than just anyone who feeds them. It also ignores the **psychodynamic** focus on security and love in human attachment; humans form attachments to people who return affection rather than people who feed them without affection. Bowlby's theory of maternal deprivation is superior in this regard.

Crucial to Bowlby's view is the idea of the CRITICAL PERIOD. Bowlby argues children cannot form meaningful attachments after the critical period (0-3 years), no matter what warmth, love and security they are offered later.

Applications

Bowlby's theory has had positive and negative applications.

On the positive side, institutions like hospitals and orphanages are now much more aware of the possible damage caused to children by maternal deprivation. Institutions train staff to interact with children and play with them and provide a stimulating environment. Although care staff work shifts, greater effort is made to ensure that child has one particular carer they can attach to. If the child has parents or family nearby, there is much more emphasis on visiting times in hospitals and allowing parents to spend the night beside their child. Provision is made for women in hospital or in prison to spend quality time with their children as often as possible

On the negative side, the focus on the maternal bond has put pressure on mothers and diminished the role of fathers. Bowlby initially believed that MONOTROPY had to involve attachment to the mother and his ideas were used to encourage many mothers to stay at home and postpone or abandon their careers or education. Women who do work or study may feel anxiety that they are damaging their children by putting them in **daycare** (*c.f.* p55).

Fathers have been neglected because of Bowlby's theories. Fathers are less likely to gain custody of children and get less leave from work to care for their children. This is partly because of sexist assumptions but partly because Bowlby's early theory has made people believe the father is unimportant in childcare. More recent research challenges this. **Freeman *et al.* (2010)** shows male children prefer their father as an attachment figure. He also finds children are more likely to be attached to their father during their late childhood to early adolescence but infants and young adults are less likely to be attached to their fathers.

Since 2010, fathers in the UK have been entitled to some paternity leave. This shows a weakening of Bowlby's theory in the minds of lawmakers.

REVISING ATTACHMENT, PRIVATION & DEPRIVATION

DEFINITIONS

ANACLITIC DEPRESSION
CRITICAL PERIOD
DEPRIVATION
ETHOLOGY
FERAL CHILD
HOSPITALISM
INTERNAL WORKING MODEL
MATERNAL DEPRIVAION
MONOTROPY
P-D-D MODEL
PRIVATION
SOCIAL RELEASER
SUPER-EGO
SURVIVAL TRAIT

RESEARCH SUMMARIES

CURTISS (1977)
HARLOW (1958)
KOLUCHOVÁ (1972)
ROBERTSON (1953)
RUTTER (1976)
SKEELS & DYE (1939) + SKEELS (1966)
SPITZ (1946)

COMPREHENSION QUESTIONS

1. Who was John Bowlby?
2. What is the theory of evolution?
3. What is imprinting?
4. What were the wire mother and the cloth mother?
5. What happened to Laura?
6. What happened to Genie?
7. What happened to Oxana Malaya?
8. What are the results of maternal deprivation in adults?
9. What evidence suggests privation is reversible?
10. What evidence suggests privation is not reversible?
11. What was the impact of Bowlby's theory on mothers?
12. What was the impact of Bowlby's theory on fathers?

RESEARCH

Find out more about the Romanian orphan crisis
(tip: use the **bbb.co.uk site** to search for 'romanian orphan')
Add news articles to your notes

- How does this story link to privation?
- How does it link to deprivation?
- What does it suggest about reversibility?

EXAM-STYLE QUESTIONS

Your neighbours are considering adopting a 3-year-old child. They are concerned that a child who grew up in an orphanage might have problems.

(a) State the meaning of deprivation. [2 marks AO1]

(b) Explain possible effects of deprivation, referring to your neighbours' plans to adopt. [4 marks AO2]

(c) Evaluate whether deprivation is reversible. [8 marks AO1+AO3]

BOWLBY'S WORK ON ATTACHMENT

You've learned a lot about Bowlby already:

- He was an English psychologist who hated his own childhood experience of being sent away to boarding school
- He combined **Lorenz's ethological model** of attachment as an instinct with **Freud's psychodynamic idea** of the intense emotional bond between a child and its mother (although he later acknowledged that the child could bond with a father or other carer)
- He proposed MONOTROPY (a single attachment between child and mother) and MATERNAL DEPRIVATION (the damage caused by breaking the monotropic bond) which can turn deprived children into *"affectionless psychopaths"*
- Bowlby thought there was a CRITICAL PERIOD for forming attachments and that a child should not be away from its mother *at all* for the first 18 months and only for short periods for the first 3-4 years)

> The phrase *'Bowlby's work on attachment" refers to his famous 1944 study **"44 Juvenile Thieves."** This study isn't named in the Specification, but you should refer to it when describing Bowlby's research.*

44 JUVENILE THIEVES (1944)

Bowlby published this famous study in 1944, but the research was carried out between 1936-9. Bowlby ran a Child Guidance Clinic in London and troubled children were sent to his clinic by schools, parents or courts.

AIM: Bowlby investigated whether there was a link between children showing delinquency and their earlier separation from their mothers.

PROCEDURE: This is a natural experiment, where the (naturally-occurring) IV is whether or not the children experienced maternal deprivation in early childhood and the DV is the degree of delinquency and emotional disorder in their later childhood and adolescence.

The sample was a group of 44 children sent to the clinic for criminal behaviour (stealing). There was a control group of 44 children attending the clinic who were emotionally disordered (e.g. some had speech impediments) but not criminal. Half the children were under age 11 but the oldest was 16; there were 31 boys and 13 girls in each group.

The children were assessed at the clinic using questionnaires and interviews with a trained psychiatrist (Bowlby); this determined their personality and emotional health. In addition, their parents (usually just the mother) were interviewed about the family situation and past history.

Bowlby recorded whether each child had experienced prolonged separation from the mother in infancy (e.g. time in a foster home). Bowlby identified the children in 6 groups:

Group	Type	Behaviour
1	Normal	Children whose behaviour seemed to be a normal reaction to difficult circumstances
2	Depressed	Quiet and reserved; behaviour seemed to be a response to the death of a family member
3	Circular	Alternating depression and over-activity (**bipolar**, by today's definitions)
4	Hyperthymic	Over-active; behaviour is linked to a need for affection and attention
5	Affectionless	No affection, shame or sense of responsibility; behaviour is linked to cruelty, defiance and deceitfulness
6	Schizoid	Psychotic symptoms: violent outbursts, delusions, hallucinations and paranoia

Bowlby also wrote up short **case studies** of children in each group to illustrate their problems and behaviour (**qualitative data**).

RESULTS: Bowlby compares the delinquent group (the 'juvenile thieves') with the control group. There were 14 'affectionless' children in the delinquent group but none in the control group. Only 2 delinquents were 'normal' but "*even these two possessed characteristics which showed instability.*" In both groups, 50% of the children had mental health problems in their family (parents or grandparents).

Bowlby describes an 'affectionless' child: Kenneth (age 12) had been placed in a loving foster-home but returned to his biological mother when he was 3; he stole from his mother from age 5 and forged cheques at age 11; he was cruel to his siblings and step-siblings (at age 7 he burned one of them for amusement); he would laugh when he made his family cry.

Bowlby then investigates the incidences of maternal separation in both groups. 40% of the delinquents had experienced separation, compared to 5% of the controls. 12 of the 14 'affectionless' delinquents had experienced separation, compared to just 5 of the other delinquents and 2 of the controls.

'Separation' often involved the child being placed with foster-parents before the age of 5 (often because the father deserted the mother or the mother became ill) then being returned to the biological mother later:

mothers have described reuniting with their children as 'like looking after someone else's baby', and described them as 'stranger' and 'the odd one out'. Such accounts are vivid evidence of the shattering effect these long separations have on the emotional bonds which usually unite mother and child – **John Bowlby**

Bowlby observes that most of these separations took place *after* the child was 1 year old.

CONCLUSIONS: Bowlby identifies a number of possible causes for the delinquency and particularly the 'affectionless' characters.

- **Genetics:** The children might have inherited this behaviour. However, as far as Bowlby could tell, mental health problems were equally present in the families in both groups
- **Parental Instability:** Bowlby notes that, of the 27 non-separated delinquents, only 7 had parents who seemed healthy and stable. The rest had either *"unstable and nagging mothers"* or *"fathers who hated them."* However, parental instability seemed equally common in the control group.
- **Later Traumatic Experiences:** Bowlby acknowledges 11 cases where the child had been through a recent trauma, such as the death of a loved one or jealousy at the birth of a new family member.
- **Separation:** Bowlby considers family breakdown in early childhood to be the biggest single factor that separates the delinquent children (and especially the 'affectionless' ones) from the controls. He concludes that separation after the first 12 months is particularly damaging – this is DEPRIVATION because the attachment bond is formed but then broken.

EVALUATING BOWLBY'S WORK ON ATTACHMENT AO3

GENERALISABILITY: The study investigates children in London in the 1930s, before the creation of the NHS or the Welfare State (which have probably improved the lives of children) and before the Internet, video games and mobile phones (which have certainly changed the lives of children, for better or worse). It is difficult to generalise the results to 21st century children, children from the countryside and children from other cultures. For example, in COLLECTIVIST cultures (e.g. in Asia) children may be cared for by an extended family of uncles, aunts and cousins.

RELIABILITY: Bowlby followed **standardised procedures** in the way the children were given questionnaires then they and their families were interviewed. However, his method for categorizing children (e.g. as 'affectionless' or 'schizoid') seems rather subjective (e.g. he thought even the 'normal' delinquents *"showed instability"* which is probably his own bias).

Bowlby could have improved this with a DOUBLE-BLIND TECHNIQUE (i.e. getting a different psychiatrist to assess the children who didn't know whether they were from the control or the delinquent group).

APPLICATION: Bowlby clearly recommends keeping families together once the baby has formed an attachment to its mother (i.e. by 12 months). This would include providing benefits to help single mothers (as we now do, but didn't in the 1930s) and making sure mothers in prison or in hospital remain in contact with their children. A more controversial application is encouraging mothers to stay at home with young children rather than work or study while their children are in daycare.

VALIDITY: A lot of the data in this study is RETROSPECTIVE (looking back to the past, *c.f.* p75) and involves parents and a child trying to remember what early childhood was like. People are not very good at remembering things like this and their memories are often distorted by their more recent experiences (e.g. if home life is terrible now, we tend to remember only the bad things from the past). **Bartlett's schema theory of memory** (*c.f.* **Cognitive Psychology**) helps explain this. However, Bowlby collects qualitative data as well as quantitative data to build up a rounded picture of these children's problems and their difficult home lives.

ETHICS: The children were being treated at the Clinic for their various problems and the research did not interfere with their treatment (indeed, the questionnaires and interviews were ***part*** of their treatment). The children were too young to give consent but their parents gave PRESUMPTIVE CONSENT (on the child's behalf) and were fully involved with the research all the way through.

Bowlby does refer to the delinquents as *"thieves"* all the way through the research: this is inaccurate (most were too young to be charged with theft, never mind convicted of it) and very judgemental. Social sensitivity in research instructs us to avoid giving participants labels like this. **Rosenhan's pseudopatient study** (*c.f.* **Clinical Psychology**) shows the danger of labelling people. However, Bowlby's research dates from before ethical guidelines were put in place.

FURTHER REFLECTIONS

> *You could be set a 16-mark essay question on 'Bowlby's work on attachment' with up to 10 marks for AO3, so you should try to go beyond the basic G-R-A-V-E evaluation points.*

Bowlby has attracted a lot of criticism over the years. **Feminists** see his theories as part of an effort in the 1950s by men to get women to give up the jobs and independence they had enjoyed during the War and return to the home.

Psychologists following **Freud**'s ideas (who were very influential in the '50s and '60s and shaped the ideas in the DSM-I and DSM-II – *c.f.* **Clinical Psychology**) rejected Bowlby for focusing on actual experiences of separation and loss rather than sexual fantasies.

Other critics observe that Bowlby tends to 'cherry pick' his quantitative data. For example, 40% of the delinquents had experienced separation – but 60% hadn't, but were still delinquent! In fact, 2 of the affectionless delinquents had no history of maternal deprivation either.

These criticisms and others were summed up by **Michael Rutter**'s 1972 book *Maternal Deprivation Reassessed*. Rutter argues that Bowlby mistook **correlation** (a link between maternal deprivation and delinquency) for **causation**, when in fact Bowlby's research doesn't show cause-and-effect. Rutter also points out that Bowlby fails to distinguish between **privation** (the total lack of attachment) and **deprivation** (the loss of earlier attachment).

However, Bowlby can be viewed in a positive light. He was one of the first people to expose the scale of emotional suffering among children who had previously been dismissed as 'wicked' or 'naughty'. Bowlby showed that these children needed *more* love, not less. Bowlby's qualitative data provides some chilling insights into families with mothers who cannot cope and fathers who are either absent or positively hateful towards their children or step-children.

Bowlby's quantitative data is more thoughtful than is often claimed. Bowlby does examine alternative explanations (such as genetics or bad parenting) and he does admit that he lacks sufficient data to assess the full impact of family histories on children. He also acknowledges that his research would have benefited from a truly healthy control group – but of course, his Clinic did not give him access to children without problems.

Because of all this, Bowlby admits that maternal deprivation is not the *only* factor causing child delinquency. He just points out that it is a *significant* factor, apparently a more significant one than the more obvious factors like genes or bad parenting – moreover, it's a factor that could be addressed by social policies that would help keep families together rather than separating infants from their mothers.

Bowlby is *not* arguing that only mothers can provide the attachment children need (despite using the term MATERNAL deprivation) and he doesn't personally argue that it's women who must stay at home and nurture children (just that *somebody* has to).

Bowlby's work had a big influence on social policy (such as providing Child Benefit to families with young children) and on other researchers: **Mary Ainsworth** carried on Bowlby's research with his support and **Michael Rutter**, although he criticised Bowlby's methods, continued to develop Bowlby's basic idea that children have an instinctive need for love and security and suffer long-term damage without it.

AINSWORTH'S WORK ON ATTACHMENT

Mary Ainsworth was an American/Canadian psychologist who met **John Bowlby** after the War and developed his research into attachment. In collaboration with her colleague **Sylvia Bell**, Ainsworth created the STRANGE SITUATION PROCEDURE (SSP) to study variations in attachment.

For Bowlby, attachment was all-or-nothing (either the child was attached or it wasn't) but Ainsworth considered different ATTACHMENT STYLES that might be partly a result of the child's personality but also a response to the way the parent treated it. There are **four key elements of child behaviour**:

1. How much does the child explore its surroundings?
2. What is the child's reaction when the parent leaves (SEPARATION ANXIETY)?
3. Does the child express **anxiety** with the introduction of a stranger when the child is alone (STRANGER ANXIETY)?
4. How does the child interact with the parent when distressed?

Ainsworth proposes that a securely-attached infant will explore its surroundings, show distress when the parent leaves and anxiety in the presence of strangers, but be calmed by the return of the parent. From this, she develops **attachment styles**:

Type	Attachment is...	Description
A	Insecure* Avoidant	This child displays AMBIVALENCE (mixed feelings) when the mother is present or not present: the child rarely clings to the caregiver and often refuses to be held; avoids exploration and displays ambivalence toward strangers (i.e. strangers treated the same as the parent)
B	Secure	Healthy strong attachment to the mother: this child will explore and engage with others when the mother is present; when the mother leaves the child will avoid contact with strangers
C	Insecure* Resistant	This child shows anxiety when a stranger is present even while the mother is there: the child will not freely explore and becomes extremely distressed when the mother is absent; when the mother returns the child is unreceptive to the mother's attempts at interaction

These styles are sometimes termed "anxious" rather than "insecure"

While securely-attached infants are curious and bold, alert to danger for easily reassured, the insecurely attached (or "*anxious*") infants behave differently.

- **Avoidant (type A) babies** are very independent: they are bold but cannot be comforted. This may be because they have not been shown love and attention and have learned to cope without it.
- **Resistant (type C) babies** are very 'clingy' but they 'punish' their caregiver when they are distressed. This may be because they have received inconsistent love or 'mixed messages' from their parent.

Ainsworth adapted the idea of the INTERNAL WORKING MODEL from Bowlby and **Melanie Klein** (p20) – the child's mental view of relationships is established by their relationship with their first carer. A securely attached child is:

likely to possess a representational model of attachment figures(s) as being available, responsive, and helpful – **John Bowlby**

Ainsworth *et al.* (1978) suggests that the carer's sensitivity is highly important (the CAREGIVER SENSITIVITY HYPOTHESIS). As the flowchart shows, the child's behaviour then reinforces the carer's behaviour (sensitive carers find their children are responsive to them, insensitive casers find their children don't respond to them).

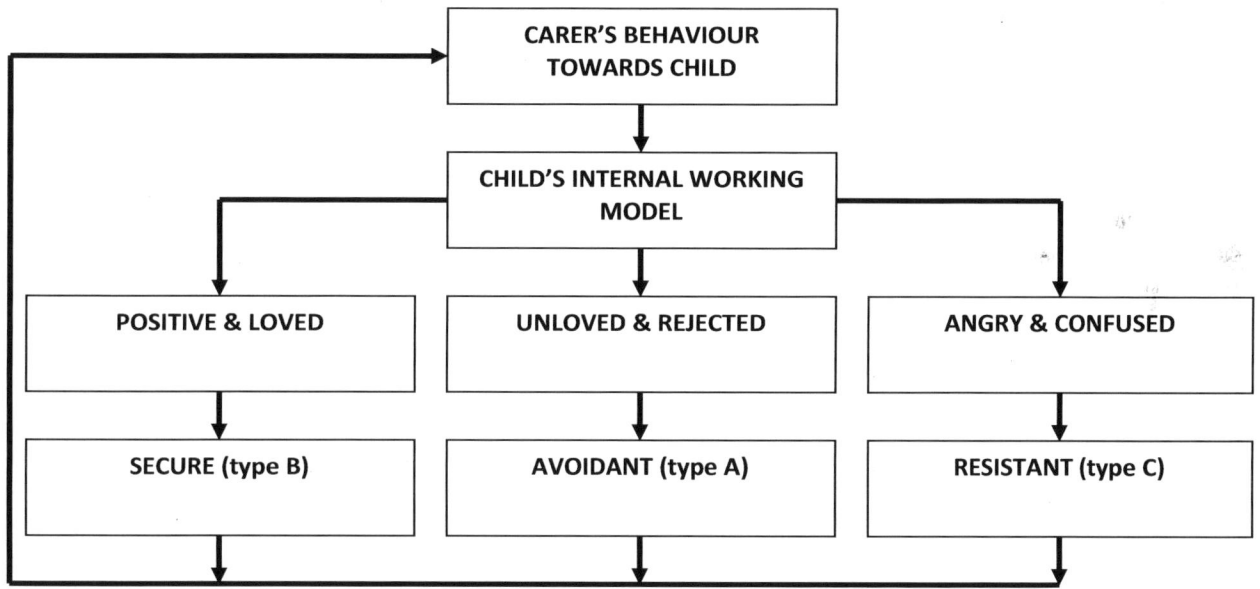

Notice how the parent's behaviour influences the child – but then the child's behaviour loops back and influences the parent. It's easy to love affectionate children and hard to show warmth towards children who reject you. This is a VICIOUS CIRCLE for carer and child.

THE STRANGE SITUATION PROCEDURE (SSP)

Ainsworth put her ideas to the test with this innovative type of **structured observation**. The SSP has since been replicated by many other researchers. The SSP was created by **Ainsworth & Wittig (1969)** based on Ainsworth's previous Uganda study (1967) and later studies in Baltimore, USA (**Ainsworth *et al.*, 1971, 1978**).

The experiment is set up in a room with a one-way mirror so the behaviour of the infant can be observed covertly.

> *Remember other studies observing people through one way mirrors?* **Milgram** *did this and so did* **Bandura**.

Infants were aged 12-18 months. Ainsworth's first Baltimore sample was taken from 26 middle-class American families. Each child was observed in series of 8 episodes lasting 3 minutes each:

1. Mother, baby, and experimenter (lasts less than one minute).
2. Mother and baby alone.
3. Stranger joins the mother and infant (STRANGER ANXIETY).
4. Mother leaves baby and stranger alone (SEPARATION ANXIETY).
5. Mother returns and stranger leaves (a REUNION EPISODE)
6. Mother leaves; infant left completely alone (SEPARATION ANXIETY).
7. Stranger returns (STRANGER ANXIETY).
8. Mother returns and stranger leaves (another REUNION EPISODE)

The researcher pays particular attention to the two reunion episodes and notes down the behaviour displayed at 15-second intervals and scores it on a 1 to 7 intensity scale.

Intensity	Proximity & contact-seeking	Contact maintaining	Proximity & interaction avoiding	Proximity & interaction resisting	Searching
1					
2		✓			
3					✓
4	✓✓				
5					✓
6	✓				
7		✓			

*Secure children will **seek** and **maintain** closeness and contact with the mother; insecure children will **avoid** contact or even **resist** it; children will **search** for the mother when she is absent*

Ainsworth (1970) identifies her three main attachment styles, secure (type B), insecure avoidant (type A) and insecure resistant (type C). She concludes that these attachment styles are the result of early interactions with the mother.

	Secure (B)	Avoidant (A)	Resistant (C)
Separation Anxiety	Distress when mother leaves	No distress when mother leaves	Intense distress when mother leaves
Stranger Anxiety	Avoidant when alone but friendly with mother present	Plays normally when stranger is present	Avoidant – shows fear of stranger
Reunion Behaviour	Positive & happy when mother returns	Little interest when mother returns	Approaches mother but resists contact – may push her away
Other Behaviour	Uses mother as safe base to explore environment	Equally comforted by mother and stranger	Cries more and explores less than other two types
Percentage	70%	15%	15%

Separation anxiety is a healthy response to the mother's absence and so is stranger anxiety – these are SURVIVAL TRAITS and SOCIAL RELEASERS that have evolved in humans

EVALUATING AINSWORTH'S WORK ON ATTACHMENT AO3

GENERALISABILITY: The research might not generalise to fathers. In particular, a child might have one sort of attachment to the mother and a different sort to the father, but Ainsworth only studied mothers. Moreover, her US sample was entirely middle class families and might not generalise to working class parents.

Ainsworth explored cultural differences in a way that Bowlby did not: her first research was with African families in Uganda, then later in America (*c.f.* p71). However, the SSP might not be a culture-fair method. In small tribal cultures, even a short period of separation from the mother might be unusual and stressful, whereas in Western society even the most attentive mothers leave their child alone briefly with other carers.

RELIABILITY: The SSP is a standardised procedure and Ainsworth was able to replicate with more American families. This makes her findings very reliable. The one-way mirror and covert observation also adds to reliability, because the child would not have reacted to the observers. The SSP has been replicated by other researchers in other cultures.

APPLICATION: Parents can use Ainsworth's findings to identify the attachment style of their child and alter their own behaviour to change the child's attachment style. For example, they could try to be more sensitive to help the child be more securely attached.

Other researchers have used Ainsworth's SSP methodology to explore attachment in more depth. For example, **Main & Solomon (1990)** identify a fourth attachment style called "disorganised" (Type D) which occurs when the child fears the parent (due to abuse or the parent's erratic behaviour).

VALIDITY: Lamb *et al.* (1985) criticise the SSP for lacking ecological validity: the child is put in a strange environment that they would never normally find themselves in. The mother and stranger entering and leaving the room follows a predetermined script which is 'stilted' and unnatural. This means the child's behaviour will be unnatural too.

ETHICS: The SSP puts the child under stress (separation and stranger anxiety), which breaks **ethical guidelines** on protection of participants. However, Ainsworth put a stop to separation episodes if the child became too stressed. **Mario Marrone (1998)** argues that the SSP simulates harmless everyday life, as mothers often leave their babies for brief periods of time in different settings and with unfamiliar people (e.g. babysitters).

FURTHER REFLECTIONS

You could be set a 16-mark essay question on 'Ainsworth's work on attachment' or on the SSP as a methodology. Since there could be up to 10 marks for AO3, so you should try to go beyond the basic G-R-A-V-E evaluation points.

Ainsworth provided the first empirical (observation-based) evidence to support Bowlby's theory of attachment and the concept of the internal working model. However, it's not clear what causes what:

- Do insensitive/unresponsive parents produce insecurely attached children?
- Do unresponsive or clingy children cause their parents to behave insensitively?

Ainsworth argues that the parents influence the children rather than *vice versa*. Critics argue that caregiver sensitivity theory places too much blame on the mother. This is a reductionist approach and has unfortunate applications (e.g. blaming mums – especially single mums – for delinquent children).

However, children with different innate (inborn) personalities might develop different attachment types regardless of how sensitive their parents are. **Nathan Fox (1989)** found that attachment style is strongly linked to how regularly babies eat and sleep and how comfortable they are with new experiences, with settled but confident children being more securely attached. This is an application of the NATURE-NURTURE DEBATE.

Belsky & Rovine (1987) propose an INTERACTIONIST (nature *and* nurture) solution: the child's attachment type is a result of both the child's innate personality *and* how the parents' sensitivity and responsiveness. They conclude that insecure children need exceptionally patient and sensitive carers who can help the child develop a secure attachment. This has implications for the 'Daycare Debate (*c.f.* p36).

REVISING BOWLBY & AINSWORTH

DEFINITIONS

AFFECTIONLESS
ATTACHMENT STYLE
AVOIDANT
CAREGIVER SENSITIVITY HYPOTHESIS
CRITICAL PERIOD
DELINQUENT
MATERNAL DEPRIVAION
MONOTROPY
RESISTANT
REUNION BEHAVIOUR
SEPARATION ANXIETY
STRANGER ANXIETY
STRANGE SITUATION

RESEARCH SUMMARIES

AINSWORTH *ET AL.* (1978)
BOWLBY (1944)
FOX (1989)
LAMB *ET AL.* (1985)
MARRONE (1998)
RUTTER (1972)

RESEARCH

Find out more about the life and work of EITHER John Bowlby OR MARY AINSWORTH

(tip: use a search engine, typing in their name + 'life')

Add details to your notes

- What are their backgrounds?
- What impact did their theories have
- How did their theories change?
- How are they viewed now?

COMPREHENSION QUESTIONS

1. Who were the 44 juvenile thieves?
2. How many thieves showed maternal deprivation?
3. What did Bowlby's participant Kenneth do?
4. How old do children have to be before they can be separated from their mother, according to Bowlby?
5. Where is Uganda?
6. What does it mean to say the mother is a 'safe base'?
7. Why does insecure attachment happen?
8. What is the difference between Type A and Type C?
9. What is Type D?
10. How does attachment style affect later life?
11. Why did Ainsworth use a one-way mirror?
12. What was a problem with Ainsworth's US sample?

EXAM-STYLE QUESTIONS

Maddi is a single mother with a 6-month-old baby boy, Jack. Maddi complains that Jack is clingy, that he screams when she is away from him and is impossible to calm.

(a) State the meaning of attachment. [2 marks AO1]

(b) Explain one strength and one weakness of the theory of maternal deprivation. [4 marks AO3]

(c) Using your knowledge of Psychology, explain Jack's behaviour and suggest what Maddi can do about it . [8 marks AO1+AO2]

RESEARCH INTO DAYCARE

Daycare is when a child is cared for, usually during working hours, by someone other than their parents or legal guardians. In the UK, the term 'nursery' is still used for child daycare to distinguish it from daycare for the elderly or the ill. Daycare frees up time for the parents of children (especially their mothers) to work or study, so this is very important for the advancement of women's rights as well as reducing poverty.

Daycare nurseries in the UK are usually open all year round, 7am-7pm. Putting a child in daycare for a week typically costs £200-300 but 3- and 4-year olds get 10-30 hours of free childcare a week from the UK Government.

The **"Daycare Debate"** turns around whether children benefit from daycare or whether they are damaged by separation from their primary carers. You already know some Psychology that has an application for this:

- Children separated from their primary carers first protest, then despair and finally become detached (**Robertson, 1953**)

- Loss of attachment can lead to hospitalism and anaclitic depression as well as the lowering of IQ (**Spitz, 1946**)

- Maternal deprivation might turn daycare children into *"affectionless psychopaths"* (**Bowlby, 1944**)

- Parents who put their children in daycare are being insensitive to their needs, which results in insecure attachment and an internal working model that makes future relationships difficult (**Ainsworth, 1978**)

- Children aged 12 months+ are capable of forming attachments to several people (**Schaffer & Emerson, 1964**) and this includes nursery carers

- Stimulation and social experiences (such as playing with other children) can actually remove the effects of early privation (**Rutter, 1976; Skeels & Dye, 1939**)

- Whether a child responds well to daycare might be down to their innate personality (**Fox, 1989**)

- Patient and sensitive carers (e.g. at nursery) can help even insecure children develop secure attachments (**Belsky & Rovine, 1987**)

However, these are all general theories of attachment and development. To settle the "Daycare Debate" it is necessary to look at research *specifically* into daycare and its effects on children.

HIGH QUALITY VS LOW QUALITY DAYCARE

Spitz's 1946 study into hospitalised children (p10) shows that, if left in an unstimulating environment without consistent carers to bond with, children deteriorate emotionally and intellectually. Spitz terms this HOSPITALISM but it can also apply in nurseries if children are "warehoused" without challenging activities and with an ever-changing roster of staff who pay little attention to them.

High Quality Daycare...	Low Quality Daycare...
Small class size + high adult-to-child ratio	Large class size + low adult-to-child ratio
Language-rich environment	Language-poor environment
Stimulating activities	Unstimulating activities
Skilled staff who respond to children with warmth	Unskilled staff who respond to children coldly
Low staff turnover	High staff turnover

In the UK, adult-to-child ratios must be 1:3 for under-2s, 1:4 for 2-3s and 1:8 for 3-7s; many argue that, for under-2s, the ratio should be as close to 1:1 as possible. IN CONTRAST a ratio of 1:10 or lower leaves children neglected by adults.

A "language-rich" environment is linked to stimulating activities and skilled staff because it involves adults talking to children, using varied vocabulary and encouraging children to respond: from age 2 children learn 10 words a day and by age 6 they have a vocabulary of 15,000 words. IN CONTRAST staff who ignore children, speak to them only to give instructions or speak to them only in "baby talk" will not improve the children's language.

"Stimulating activities" stretch children cognitively and socially and include games, puzzles, group activities (like singing) and tasks encouraging curiosity and problem-solving. These include activities that build vocabulary and maths skills as well as music and art. IN CONTRAST leaving children to watch TV or play video games is not stimulating.

"Skilled staff" in the UK have at least GCSEs but 66% of nurseries employed at least one graduate (NVQ Level 3) in 2016 (though this figure is dropping). UK staff turnover is 15% each year but in nurseries it can be 30-40%. IN CONTRAST low wages and long hours mean many staff leave looking for better pay and since 89% of nursery staff are female they sometimes leave to start their own families. **Melhuish (2004)** noticed increased aggression among children whose carers were constantly changing.

IN CONCLUSION: High-quality daycare will have staffing ratios of 1:8 or less, staff trained to GCSE or above (with at least one graduate) offering language-rich and stimulating activities and with a staff turnover rate of 15% or less.

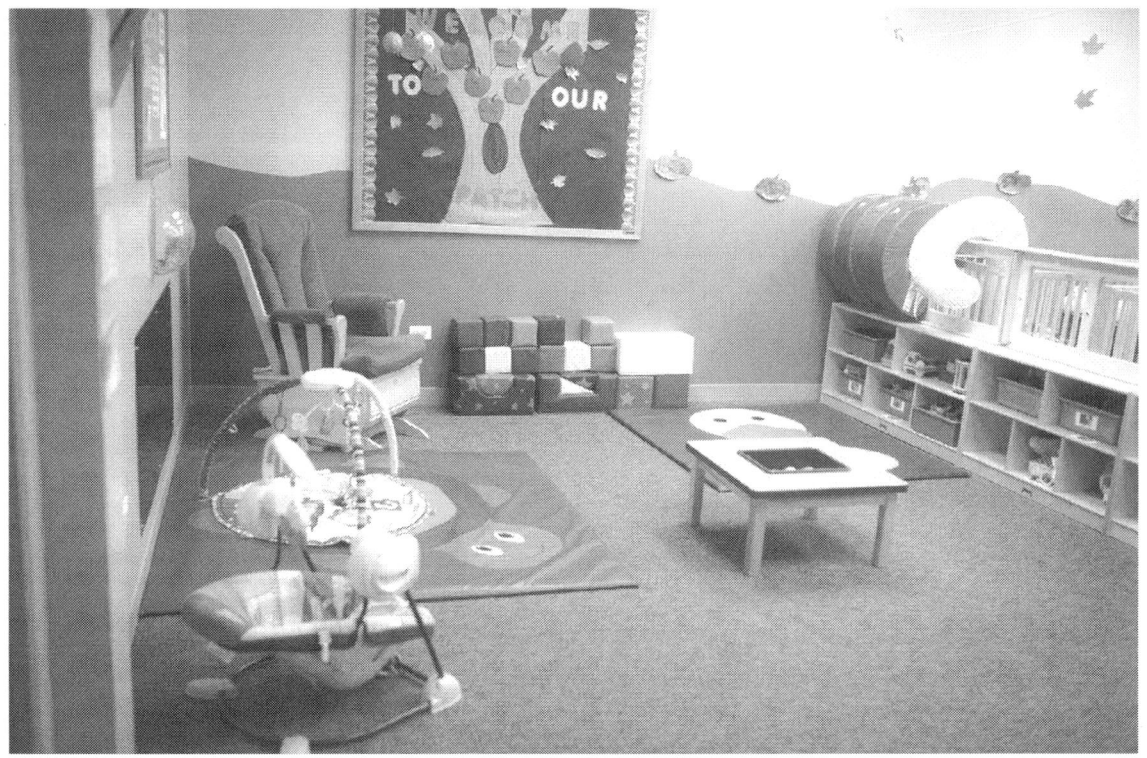

Kids Work Chicago Daycare (kidsworkchicago.com): what indications of high-quality daycare can you see here?

JAY BELSKY "INFANT DAYCARE: A CAUSE FOR CONCERN?"

Jay Belsky (1986) sounded the first warnings about possible risks of daycare for children, particularly making them more aggressive in later childhood and adolescence. These risks were particularly great if:

- Daycare began when the child was in the first year of life
- The child received more than 20 hours/week of daycare
- Daycare was continuous right up until school-age

Obviously, this leaves many children unharmed who start daycare later (after becoming securely attached at home), who do not spend too long in daycare (so that their bond with their parents is not broken) and who get 'holidays' from daycare.

Belsky & Rovine (1988) studied 149 infants (90 boys, 59 girls) who were the firstborn children of married middle class families in the USA. They **interviewed** the families about the daycare they used when the children were 3 months old, 9 months and 12 months.

When the children were 12 months old, they carried out **Ainsworth's Strange Situation Procedure** (SSP, p32). However, unlike Ainsworth, they carried out the SSP with first the mother *then* a month later with father too.

More children in full-time daycare (35+ hours per week) were insecurely attached (47%) than those with little or no daycare (25%). 20 hours of daycare a week seemed to be the 'cut-off point' for secure attachment. In particular, boys in full-time daycare were less securely attached to their fathers.

Mothers of insecurely-attached infants showed less sensitivity and empathy in interviews and expressed unhappiness in their marriages; they said that their infants were more fussy and difficult at the 3 months stage.

NICHD STUDY IN THE USA (SECCYD)

Belsky's study was very controversial (Belsky claims he was eventually 'forced out' of the USA for his unpopular views and has since worked in the UK) but it prompted the US Government to investigate further. Between 1991-2009, the **National Institute for Child Health & Human Development (NICHD)** worked with Belsky to conduct a **longitudinal study** (p75) which used observations, interviews and surveys to follow 1,200 infants from birth, until they started school. This was the **Study of Early Child Care & Youth Development (SECCYD)**.

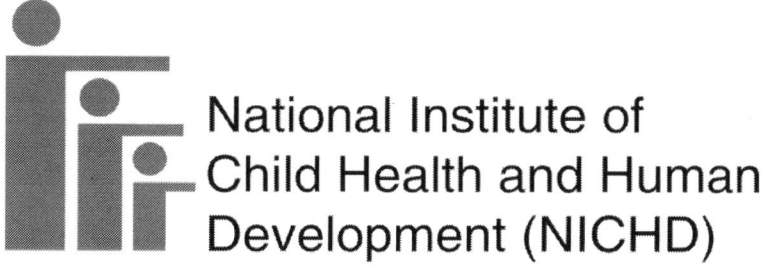

National Institute of Child Health and Human Development (NICHD)

These were the SECCYD findings:

- **Quality of daycare:** low quality daycare is bad for children whose mothers lack sensitivity; high quality daycare improves cognitive development
- **Length of daycare:** children spending early (before 12 months), continuous (right up to school-age) and intensive (20+ hours per week) time in daycare were more likely to develop behavioural problems. Children in full-time daycare (35+ hours per week) were almost 3 times more likely to show behavioural problems (tantrums, lying, hitting) than children brought up at home.
- **Type of daycare:** nursery-type daycare improves language and cognitive development, but also increases behavioural problems; in contrast, care in someone's home (i.e. a childminder or nanny) has the opposite effect

In the late 1990s, the NICHD studies concluded that the more time children spent in childcare, irrespective of its quality, the more aggressive and disobedient they were between two and six years old, especially so for group care – **Jay Belsky**

Belsky admits that most of the differences are small but warns that these effects are a "*slow, steady trickle*" that will increase as more and more families (encouraged by the Government) put their children into daycare.

EPPE PROJECT IN THE UK

All these studies were in the USA, which was the first country to embark on wide scale daycare for children. With the UK set to follow the American approach, the UK Government launched the **EPPE project (Effective Provision of Pre-school Education)**. This was another **longitudinal study** led by **Kathy Sylva *et al.* (1997-2003)**. The sample included 3000 children aged 3-11 from a range of backgrounds (race, religion, social class, etc). There were two groups: children attending daycare and children at home (the Control Group).

Sylva found that high quality daycare improved social, cognitive and behavioural development. Moreover, the earlier a child started daycare, the bigger the improvement. Children who had been in daycare longer had better social skills, concentration and independence. This was particularly the case for children from disadvantaged backgrounds, for whom part-time daycare was just as beneficial as full-time daycare.

KOREN-KARIE ON INSECURE PARENTS

Most of this research suggests that daycare is responsible for how children turn out, but **Nina Koren-Karie (2001)** controversially challenges this assumption. She suggests that insecure parents are more likely to put their children into daycare, meaning that daycare classes are disproportionately full of insecurely-attached children.

Koren-Karie tested 76 Israeli mothers (mean age 27): 38 using nursery daycare while they returned to work, 38 remaining at home on maternity leave. Both groups were matched on age and social class.

Koren-Karie **interviewed** the mothers using the **Adult Attachment Interview (AAI)** to determine their attachment type. The AAI is a **structured interview** technique (p63, *c.f.* p90) that has 20 pre-written questions (e.g. "*Choose five adjectives or words that reflect your relationship with your mother*"). It reveals the respondent's INTERNAL WORKING MODEL (p20), which shows how attached they were to their parents and the sort of attachments they form with their children.

The securely attached mothers mostly chose to care for their babies at home. However, more of the insecurely-attached mothers chose to use daycare. This suggests that maternal characteristics are responsible for the insecurely-attached infants in daycare.

EVALUATING RESEARCH INTO DAYCARE AO3

GENERALISABILITY: Belsky & Rovine (1989) used only married, middle-class Americans in their sample, which might not generalise to single parents, working classes and non-Americans. By contrast, the **EPPE Project** included a diverse sample in terms of race and class and generalises better to British families.

The **SECCYD** also has a large and more representative sample (but might not be representative of British families and daycare). **Koren-Karie (2001)** used an Israeli sample which might be very different culturally from both the USA and the UK.

RELIABILITY: These studies use standardised procedures. **Belsky & Rovine (1989)** use the tried-and-tested SSP; longitudinal studies replicate their procedures several times during their duration. However, interviews are the hardest method to replicate reliably. For example, **Koren-Karie (2001)** uses structured interviews but the interviewer might have to improvise if the interviewee doesn't understand or can't think of an answer.

APPLICATIONS: There are applications for this research for parents, who need to decide whether or not to put their children in daycare (EPPE says they should) and whether they should pay more for high-quality daycare (almost all studies say they should). There are applications for child-carers in how to set up nurseries, recruit and train staff and how to plan activities that are stimulating for children as well as the possible side-effects to watch out for. There are also applications for governments, who must decide whether to offer financial assistance to families choosing to put children in daycare (as the UK Government does) or to improve maternity and paternity benefits so that families an care for children at home.

VALIDITY: The longitudinal studies cover development in rich detail, which is valid, but there is such huge variety in types of daycare, family arrangements and children's personalities and abilities that conclusions drawn from them might not be valid. However, other studies (e.g. **Sammons *et al.*, 1994**; **Barglow *et al.*, 1987**) back up the finding that 20+ hours per week is the point at which daycare starts to show negative side-effects on some children. Moreover, all these studies are supported by research into monotropy by **Bowlby** and the **ethological** tradition of **Harlow** that shows humans have evolved to form attachments and that infants do not develop properly if these attachments are broken or interrupted.

ETHICS: As usual, the children in these studies could not consent so the parents' presumptive consent was obtained. Most of these studies only observed things the children would have been experiencing anyway (i.e. they were **natural experiments**) but some (SECCYD, EPPE) organised cognitive tests for the children (e.g. on vocabulary, arithmetic, problem-solving) which could have been stressful for them. The bigger problem is that this research is **socially sensitive**, as discussed next.

You could be set a 16-mark essay question on "research into daycare". Since there could be up to 10 marks for AO3, so you should try to go beyond the basic G-R-A-V-E evaluation points.

The research on daycare seems contradictory. Some of it suggests problems, some suggests benefits: most suggests both, with children benefiting in terms of cognitive and social skills (especially those from poorer backgrounds and experiencing high-quality care) but suffering emotionally (especially those who start daycare early and experience it full-time or being in low-quality daycare).

The debate over daycare is SOCIALLY SENSITIVE (p110) because it can alarm parents and cause them to make decisions with far-reaching consequences for their children:

- Families who reject daycare will need to have someone staying at home as a carer. This restricts family income (and poverty is more damaging for children than daycare on any measure) and the responsibility falls disproportionately on women
- Families who choose daycare may achieve benefits for women and their children but run the risk of damaging children emotionally; high-quality daycare reduces this risk but comes at a cost some families cannot afford

Jay Belsky argues that this social sensitivity produces a backlash against anyone researching the downside of daycare. Belsky claims he was driven out of the USA for his views, because child psychology is dominated by a *"liberal progressive feminist bias [whose] concern is not to make mothers feel bad!"*

Other psychologists accuse Belsky of overreacting. The EPPE Project did not support his worst predictions **Kathy Sylva** notes that any increase in aggression in children who had been through daycare had disappeared by the time they were 11.

In fact, both Belsky and Silva take a similar INTERACTIONIST view that child development is a mixture of environment, parenting and the child's own personality.

> *Children's development is shaped by many, many different factors. If the child is a healthy child, in a family that is supportive and caring and goes to a high-quality childcare setting, the evidence is that the child is not at risk* – **Kathy Sylva**

This still leaves the possibility that daycare could be damaging if it was low-quality or the child was insecure and from an unsupportive family background.

The debate continues because daycare is a growing trend. In 1981, only 24% of women returned to work after childbirth; this increased to 67% in 2001 and 80% in 2014 (source: National Childbirth Trust). This leads one psychologist to warn that:

> *[Daycare] could be the greatest social experiment of our time, in which millions of parents are unwitting participants* – **Stanley Greenspan**

AUTISM

Autism is a DEVELOPMENTAL DISORDER which causes children to develop abnormally. Autistic children have difficulty communicating and forming relationships with other people, including their own parents. They often retreat into 'a world of their own' and engage in very repetitive behaviour, which can turn into an "*insistence of same-ness*" and distress when they are exposed to change.

The most important symptoms of autism are:

- **Language deficit:** autistic children are slower to learn language and struggle with its nuances (e.g. detecting sarcasm); they often cope by repeating ('echoing') language
- **Social deficit:** autistic children have difficulty with relationships and can be identified by their failure to make eye contact or play with others
- **Behavioural Abnormalities:** These can include repetitive behaviour, obsessive routines and heightened sensitivity to sound, touch or smell; autistic children can be identified by their failure to engage in 'dress up' or 'pretend play'

Autism was first diagnosed by **Leo Kanner** in 1943. Kanner described case studies of 11 American children with unusual behaviours. For example, 5-year-old Donald liked to spin round in circles and spin his toys but would throw tantrums if his routine was interrupted. Kanner realised these children were not 'retarded' (as had previously been thought) but suffered from a syndrome (a collection of symptoms) he termed 'autism'.

Around the same time, **Hans Asperger** identified the same syndrome in 4 Austrian boys who showed "*a lack of empathy, little ability to form friendships, one-sided conversation, intense absorption in a special interest, and clumsy movements.*" Asperger termed children "*little professors*" because of their ability to talk about their favorite subject in great detail.

Weirdly, Kanner and Asperger never met and never referred to each other's work. Today, Autism and Aspergers as regarded as part of the same syndrome, with Aspergers indicating children who are 'high-functioning' but still abnormal.

Kanner proposed that autism was caused by a lack of maternal warmth (the "*refrigerator mother*") which meant the child did not form an attachment. **Bruno Bettelheim (1967)** notoriously blamed 'cold parenting': based on his claims to have observed the parents of autistic children, he compared an autistic child to a prisoner in a concentration camp and the parents to SS guards; he suggested that autistic children 'withdrew' in response to the unloving family situation.

This link between autism and attachment seems to confuse cause-and-effect. Even though autism doesn't become obvious until the child is 2, it seems to be present from birth and lack of attachment is the *result* of autism, not the *cause* of it. Bettelheim's work is now discredited (the man was a fraud and a psychopath) and parents are no longer blamed for causing autism in their children (indeed, 'cold parenting' may be a coping mechanism for parents with severely autistic children).

FEATURES OF AUTISM

When the Exam Board uses the term 'features' of a disorder, they do NOT mean 'symptoms'. Features are the general facts about the disorder: how common it is, who gets it and at what age, what it is classified as and how long it lasts.

Autism affects about 1% of the population. There are 700,000 persons with autism in the UK. It is a lifelong condition which can be treated but which has no cure. Autism is found in every country and region of the world and in families of all racial, ethnic and economic backgrounds.

Autism seems to affect males more than females. The National Autistic Society reports male-to-female ratios of 3:1 among adults and 5:1 among children (usually averaged as 4:1 overall).

However, it might be that autism is just UNDER-DIAGNOSED in females (i.e. there are just as many autistic females as males but they show symptoms differently).

Autism begins in childhood but continues into adulthood. It can be very restricting. Only 16% of autistic adults in the UK are in full-time employment and only 32% in paid work.

About half of autistic people also suffer from a learning disability (IQ less than 70), but half do not. However, autistic savants can possess 'islets of ability' in which they are exceptional. According to **Rimlaud (1978)**, savantism occurs in about 10% of autistic people and often takes the form of exceptional abilities in mathematics, music, art or memory feats.

BIOLOGICAL EXPLANATION: EXTREME MALE BRAIN

> *The Exam will ask you about "one biological explanation" of autism, not Extreme Male Brain or Simon Baron-Cohen specifically*

The idea that autism is linked to extreme male ways of thinking was suggested by **Hans Asperger** in 1944:

> *The autistic personality is an extreme variant of male intelligence ... In the autistic individual, the male pattern is exaggerated to the extreme* – **Hans Asperger**

Simon Baron-Cohen (2002) researched this link between the cause of autism and its higher frequency in males. This is the idea that autism is produced by the EXTREME MALE BRAIN (EMB). Baron-Cohen suggests that **sex differences** can be divided into:

- **Empathising (E):** having empathy (an understanding of other people's mental states)
- **Systemising (S):** organising things into systems or developing to understand thing

Males have a tendency towards systemizing but females have a tendency towards empathising. Baron-Cohen defines the "female brain" as **E>S** (or **Type E**) and the "male brain" as **S>E** (or **Type S**).

> *It's important to grasp that not everyone who is biologically female will have the classic "female brain" and the same for males. Some males may be more Type E than Type S.*

Some people will be equally good at empathising and systemising: this is **S=E**, the 'balanced brain' (or **Type B**). However, some people will be HYPER-SYSTEMISING (high levels of systemising) but HYPO-EMPATHISING (low empathy, which Baron-Cohen terms *"mind-blindness"*) and he terms this extreme version way of thinking **S>>E**, the "extreme male brain."

Baron-Cohen supposes there might be people with the "extreme female brain" who are *"systems blind"* but with hyper-developed empathising skills, termed **E>>S**.

> *The "extreme female brain" doesn't get as much attention because it doesn't mark you out as abnormal: you can get along in society just fine as a hyper-empathiser, even if you can't grasp basic maths or how to wire a plug. Remind you of anyone?*

Baron-Cohen points out sex differences that illustrate Type E and Type S thinking:

- **Sharing & turn-taking:** Girls show more concern than boys for fairness and harmony when playing, which is E>S (**Charlesworth & Dzur, 1987**)
- **Rough-and-tumble play:** Boys show more willingness to hurt their playmates and ignore their feelings, which is S>E (**Maccoby, 1998**)
- **Toy preference:** Boys are more interested than girls in building blocks and mechanical toys (vehicles, weapons), which is S>E (**Jennings, 1977**)
- **Sensitivity to facial expressions:** Women score higher than men at decoding facial expressions in tests, which is E>S (**Hall, 1978**)
- **Mental rotation test:** Males have more aptitude for puzzles involving rotating 3-D shapes in their mind; this is INPUT-OPERATION-OUTPUT thinking which is S>E (**Collins & Kimmura, 1997**)
- **Disorders of empathy:** Psychopathic disorders are more common among males as is aggression and murder (which Baron-Cohen calls *"the ultimate example of lack of empathy"*)

> *Don't worry about all these "sub-studies": just learn one or two to back up Baron-Cohen's ideas about Type E and Type S brains.*

Baron-Cohen tested autistic persons against average male and female patterns:

- **Empathy Quotient Scale (EQS):** This questionnaire measures Type E thinking and Baron-Cohen found that, on average, males score lower than females and autistic people score lowest of all (take the EQS test yourself at **discovermyprofile.com/eqs/introduction.html**)
- **Reading the Mind in the Eyes Test:** This test asks respondents to identify emotions from a "letterbox" photograph showing just the eyes; males scored lower than females and autistic people scored lowest of all (test yourself at **socialintelligence.labinthewild.org**)

What emotion is this?

- **Language Development:** Girls develop language skills earlier than boys and children with autism develop language skills very late or not at all

Baron-Cohen also points out that hyper-systemising thought might explain the "islets of ability" in autistic savants. A tendency towards systemising explains hobbies like collecting or interests in *"closed systems"* like computers which attract young boys and appeal strongly to people with autism.

There might be a biological basis for these differences. Brain structures that are on average are smaller in males than in females (e.g. the corpus callosum, prefrontal cortex and thalamus) are even smaller in people with autism; structures that are bigger in males (e.g. the amygdala) are bigger still in people with autism. On average, the male brain is larger than female brains and people with autism have even larger brains than typical males.

> *Please note that the myth that autism is caused by a biological reaction to childhood vaccines has been thoroughly debunked.*

Baron-Cohen claims that FOETAL TESTOSTERONE LEVELS have a **positive correlation** with more extreme autistic symptoms. Testosterone is the male growth hormone and exposure to testosterone in the womb causes the foetus to develop into a boy. Baron-Cohen proposes that if the foetus is exposed to too much testosterone, it develops an extreme male brain.

This can be tested because many pregnant women provide samples of amniotic fluid (the fluid surrounding the unborn child in the womb) as part of health check-ups and this sample can be tested for testosterone levels. **Chapman *et al.* (2006**, Baron-Cohen was part of this study) tested 200 pregnant mothers this way and later measured the child's empathising skills at age 6-8. They found a negative correlation between testosterone levels in the womb and things like eye contact and social relationships; in other words, the higher the testosterone, the less eye contact children made and the harder they found social relationships.

Strengths	Weaknesses
Supported by well-researched sex differences and the patterns of test scores found in autistic persons	Doesn't explain autism in females or allow for the possibility that much female autism may be undiagnosed
Supported by correlation between foetal testosterone and poor empathising	Correlations do not prove causation and other factors may be at work
Rivito (1985) found a 96% concordance with MZ twins for autism but only 23% for DZ twins, suggesting a biological link	Concordances in twin studies on autism are always less than 100%, so it's not entirely biological and environment plays a part
Brain structures that are larger or smaller in males are even more exaggerated in autistic people	Not all autistic people have these enlarged or reduced brain structures (e.g. **Bishop *et al.*, 1997**)

ANOTHER EXPLANATION: THEORY OF MIND

> *The Exam will ask you about "another explanation" or perhaps "a non-biological explanation"*
> *of autism, not Theory of Mind or Simon Baron-Cohen specifically*

Theory of Mind (ToM) is the ability to understand that other people have minds that are different from our own. In particular, it involves understanding that other people have their own thoughts, feelings and perspectives. ToM allows us to understand and predict the other people's behaviours based on what we think **they** might be thinking.

> *You probably see how ToM links to empathising: even if we're not feeling sad ourselves, if we*
> *can imagine another person's perspective we will understand they might be having a hard day.*

The classic test for ToM is the SALLY-ANNE TASK. This is a 'thought experiment' that tests a child's ability to understand and predict false beliefs. The child is shown two models ('Sally' and 'Anne' – they are usually dolls). Sally places an object (like a marble) in a hiding place and then leaves. Anne moves the object to a new hiding place. When Sally returns, the child must predict where Sally will look for the object.

1. Sally as a basket, Anne has a box

2. Sally puts her marble in her basket

3. Sally goes away, Anne moves the marble to her box

4. Sally comes back: where will she look for her marble?

- The child knows that Anne has moved the object to a new hiding place
- Sally doesn't know this: she has a FALSE BELIEF that the object is still where she left it

If the child understands false beliefs, they will predict Sally will look for the object where she left it (and find it's gone); if the child doesn't understand false beliefs, they will predict Sally will look for the object where they know Anne has hidden it.

Children under 4 often make mistakes in the Sally-Anne Task (i.e. they predict Sally will look where Anne has hidden the object), but get it consistently right by the time they are 6 (predicting that Sally will look for the object where she left it). **Baron-Cohen et al. (1985)** tested 27 healthy 4-year olds (the Control Group) and compared them to 20 11-year-olds with autism (whose average mental age was 5) and 14 10-year-olds with Down's Syndrome (whose average mental age was 2 but with no emotional problems).

	Autistic	Down's syndrome	Controls
Prediction	20%	86%	85%

The fact that the Down's Syndrome children had the same success rate in the Sally-Anne Task as the Control Group of normal 4-year-olds shows that passing the test is not related to intelligence. Only 20% of the autistic children could successfully predict where Sally would look and this suggests that this COGNITIVE DEFICIT (mental failure) is a distinctive feature of autism. In other words, the autistic children lack ToM and this is what separates them from normal children and other children with low IQ.

- **Language deficit:** without ToM, learning language is difficult since the child does not recognise language reveals another person's beliefs or perspective
- **Social deficit:** lack of ToM results in poor empathy and a tendency to find out peoples behaviour confusing which leads to inappropriate emotions
- **Behavioural Abnormalities:** Lack of ToM would explain the absence of 'dress up' or 'pretend play' in autistic children (who do not easily imagine that they are someone else or that a doll or teddy has a personality of its own)

Strengths	Weaknesses
ToM provides a single cognitive deficit underlying the varied symptoms of autism	ToM does not explain all symptoms of autism (e.g. spinning)
ToM can help parents and teachers understand autistic children because it makes their behaviour reasonable	Autistic children often excel at INPUT-OPERATION-OUTPUT tasks like computing which is not explained by ToM
ToM is backed up by 'false belief' tests like the Sally-Anne Task	Some autistic people can pass 'false belief' tests (e.g. 20% in **Baron-Cohen et al., 1985**)
ToM ties in with biological explanations like the Extreme Male Brain (EMB)	It's not clear that females have a better ToM than males

EVALUATING EXPLANATIONS OF AUTISM AO3

> *You could be asked short questions about the strengths & weaknesses of two explanations, but a 16-mark essay question on "explanations of autism' would have up to 10 marks for AO3, so you should try to go beyond the basic strengths and weaknesses.*

Research into explanations of autism is SOCIALLY SENSITIVE because it has huge implications for children and their families. If research conclusions are wrong (or just badly stated and misinterpreted), then autistic children will not be educated properly or given the help they need and families will be put under great stress.

A good example of this is the notorious 'cold parenting' theory of **Bruno Bettelheim** in the 1960s (p44). Bettelheim argued that autistic children were normal children who had been badly parented: with a little more love, they'd be fine. This caused well-meaning parents to feel extreme guilt and autistic children were treated for a problem they didn't have (lack of love) and not for one they did have (perhaps, lack of Theory of Mind).

Modern researchers (such as **Simon Baron-Cohen**'s Autism Research Unit in Cambridge) are much more mindful of this. Baron-Cohen argues that his theories of EMB and ToM hep us to sympathise with autistic people, to see the world as they see it and view their condition as less strange and threatening.

However, his work has been criticised for emphasising the differences between people with autism and everyone else, rather than the similarities. Baron-Cohen presents autism as EGOCENTRIC. For psychologists, this term means 'viewing the world from only your own perspective' but in everyday language it means 'arrogant' or 'selfish'. Baron-Cohen's theories can be misinterpreted as suggesting that autistic people are selfish and immoral and this encourages discrimination against them.

> *The idea that people with autism lack empathy is wrong. People with autism can feel others' pain, but they are slower to process this emotion* **– David Skuse**

A lot of research into children with autism is hard to **generalise** onto adults. Many adults with autism learn to show empathy and have ToM, but they do need to learn this rather than finding it natural. The Sally-Anne Task is far too simplistic to test adults (adults with autism pass it easily) so more complex tests are needed to explore ToM in adults.

Research into foetal testosterone levels is hard to generalise to autistic persons since it is only a **correlation** with **naturally-occurring variables**. All it ever shows is a link between testosterone and autism-like characteristics (e.g. lack of eye contact, social awkwardness), not a link with autism itself.

> *You're dying to know: is Simon Baron-Cohen connected to the comedian and film star Sacha Baron Cohen? YES! They are cousins, but Simon Baron-Cohen is hyphenated (from a misspelling on his first published article that he has never bothered to correct)*

THERAPIES FOR AUTISM

Since autism is a lifelong condition with no cure, there is no 'treatment' for autism that can make it go away. Instead, therapies can help autistic people manage their life better and cope with problems successfully.

Cognitive Behavioural Therapy (CBT)

CBT is a counselling technique that helps clients to identify negative thoughts, beliefs or attitudes to situations. By changing their beliefs, the client changes how they behave in that situation in future. It is very effective for treating anxiety and children with autism often suffer from anxiety in social situations. CBT needs to be adapted for children with autism, because they often have problems recognising emotions or thinking about hypothetical situations. CBT for autism focuses instead on visual cues. For example, many autistic children struggle to rate their anxiety on a '1 to 10' scale, but find it easier to think of something concrete like a thermometer getting hotter or a bucket filling with water.

Applied Behaviour Analysis (ABA)

ABA uses POSITIVE REINFORCEMENT and observes a person's communication style in order to work out the best way of changing it. Autistic children have problems interacting with others and ABA rewards them for showing improved behaviour, while unhelpful behaviour is not reinforced. The therapy provides opportunities to practise skills, with the therapist making changes improve the child's behaviour next time. This means ABA provides a "tailored programme" for each child.

EVALUATING THERAPIES FOR AUTISM AO3

These therapies are supported by research that suggests they are effective:

- **Cohen et al. (2006)** compared 21 autistic children receiving ABA with 21 in special school classes (the Control Group): 17 of the ABA group were able to return to normal school lessons compared to just 1 in the Control Group
- **Sofronoff *et al.* (2005)** surveyed parents and found that autistic children had less anxiety and better coping strategies after a brief CBT session. The CBT was even more effective if the parents took part in the session.

Autism is a syndrome with many symptoms (some children with autism have good language skills while others cannot communicate at all). These therapies work best with 'high-functioning' autistic children. However ABA can be 'tailored' around a child's particular symptoms. A criticism of ABA is that it directs the child, taking away autonomy (choice), but CBT focuses on helping children make better choices.

NATURE VS NURTURE IN ATTACHMENT

The topics so far have tended to treat attachment as something UNIVERSAL affecting all children all over the world in the same way. They also focus heavily on the NURTURE side of the nature-nurture debate because they view the child as a 'blank slate' (*tabula rasa*) who learns all attachments from his or her environment. If we take this view, then there is a fixed way all humans are supposed to turn out and if any develop abnormally then the fault must lie in their upbringing (either their parents or their daycare).

- **Schaffer & Emerson (1964)** provide a timeline for child development with **stages** that apply for all children
- **Bowlby (1944)** suggests every child needs to form a MONOTROPIC BOND with their mother (he later included fathers); there is a CRITICAL PERIOD (the first 3-4 years of life, especially the first 18 months) when this has to happen
- **Ainsworth (1978)** suggests children learn their attachment styles from their parents (the CAREGIVER SENSITIVITY HYPOTHESIS)
- **Baron-Cohen (1985)** argues that children develop a THEORY OF MIND between age 4-6 that enables them to learn language and empathise with others

However, you have been introduced to some research that contradicts the idea of universal, nurture-based child development:

- **Fox (1989)** suggests that children have their own **temperaments** which determine how they respond to their carers and the attachment styles they form
- **Belsky & Rovine (1989)** argue for an INTERACTIONIST view, that children are born with their own temperament but this then interacts with what they experience at daycare, either for better or worse
- **Baron-Cohen (2006)** proposes that autism comes about because of exposure to **foetal testosterone levels**, not parenting or infant experiences

CROSS-CULTURAL RESEARCH INTO ATTACHMENT TYPES

When we study children, we tend to study the children of our *own* culture (since they are conveniently on hand in nearby daycare centres, schools and homes). It is tempting to assume that children who are brought up in other cultures will be no different but this bias in thinking is ETHNOCENTRISM (the tendency to treat your own culture as the normal or natural one).

- **Freud** and **Bowlby** both made sweeping generalisations about all children everywhere based on studying a small number of families from their home city (Vienna and London) so this is **ethnocentric**
- **Ainsworth** studied children and parents in Kampala (Uganda, East Africa) before moving to Baltimore (USA) so this is CROSS-CULTURAL RESEARCH

- **Van Ijzendoorn & Kroonenberg (1988)** carried out a cross-cultural **meta-analysis** (review of studies) into attachment styles in different countries.

It follows from Ainsworth's idea that children learn their attachment style from their parents that children in other cultures will tend to form different attachment styles. This means the 'normal' and 'healthy' **Type B** attachment might not really be normal or particularly healthy: it's just the style we prefer in Britain and America.

This means that labelling **Type A** and **C** as 'insecure' and 'unhealthy' might just reflect our biases. In other cultures, these attachment styles will be viewed as normal and desirable:

- Some cultures (e.g. Germany) value independence and individualism and don't raise their children to be overly attached (**Type A** is more 'normal')
- Others (e.g. Japan) value dependency and a close mother-child bond (**Type C** is more 'normal')

APPLICATION – *Kibbutzim:* A *kibbutz* is a collective farm in Israel. On a traditional *kibbutz*, all the children are raised together and don't have a lot of contact with their biological parents. Instead, they are raised by caregivers and all sleep together. This provides an opportunity for psychologists to study a radically different sort of upbringing.

Children on a *kibbutz* in 1946 (source: National Photo Collection of Israel)

Because the children are apart from their mothers, **Type A attachment** makes them very independent; however, life on a *kibbutz* is COLLECTIVIST (individuality is not encouraged) so this encourages **Type C attachment** as does the lack of exposure to strangers on these remote farms. People raised in traditional *kibbutzim* sometimes have mixed feelings about their childhood: they experienced freedom but also a lack of emotional warmth.

DEVELOPMENT & ATTACHMENT

Schaffer & Emerson (1964) carried out a **longitudinal study** on 60 babies from a working class area of Glasgow, observing them in their homes, every month from birth to 18 months. The researchers noted how the babies interacted with their carers and then interviewed the carers themselves. They also asked the mother to keep a diary. Three behaviours were measured:

- **Stranger Anxiety:** how does the baby react to the arrival of a stranger?
- **Separation Anxiety:** how distressed is the baby when the carer leaves and how much comfort does it need when the carer returns?
- **Social Referencing:** how much does the baby look at their carer to check how they should react to something new (i.e. is the carer a "secure base")?

Schaffer & Emerson discovered a clear sequence that all the babies followed:

STAGE / Age	Type of Attachment
ASOCIAL / 0-6 weeks	Babies respond in a similar way to people and objects (but prefer to look at human-like things); lots of stimuli (social or non-social) will produce a smile
DIFFUSE / up to 6 months	Babies enjoy human company but respond to any human who offers stimulation or comfort (INDISCRIMINATE ATTACHMENT). From 3 months, babies smile more at familiar faces and are more easily comforted by regular caregivers
SINGLE STRONG ATTACHMENT / up to 12 months	Babies show a strong preference for a single caregiver and start to show STRANGER ANXIETY and SEPARATION ANXIETY, although some show this anxiety much more than others
MULTIPLE ATTACHMENTS / 12 months +	Babies become increasingly independent and form attachments to several people (by 18 months, they may have up to 5 attachment figures, such as siblings, grandparents and neighbours)

Babies form attachments with carers who respond to the baby's signals (a carer who shows SENSITIVE RESPONSIVENESS), not necessarily the person the baby spends a lot of time with or even the person who feeds the baby.

Securely attached infants have mothers who respond quickly to their needs and interact with them. Infants who are weakly attached are those with mothers who don't interact.

These findings link to **Harlow**'s research on monkeys and the importance of comfort in attachment as well as **Spitz**'s findings about the importance of stimulation for hospitalised children. **Ainsworth**'s CAREGIVER SENSITIVITY HYPOTHESIS is based on this.

INDIVIDUAL DIFFERENCES IN ATTACHMENT

'Individual differences' tends to mean PERSONALITY. **Belsky & Rovine (1989)** suggest that different attachment styles might be as much to do with the child's personality as the parents' sensitivity. **Nathan Fox (1989)** links three 'TEMPERAMENTS' (broad personality types) observed in babies by other researchers to **Ainsworth's Type A/B/C attachment styles**:

- **'Easy' babies:** 40% of infants eat and sleep regularly and accept new experiences comfortably; they tend to develop secure (Type B) attachments
- **'Slow to warm up' babies:** 50% of infants take time to get used to new experiences; they tend to develop insecure-avoidant (Type A) attachments
- **'Difficult' babies:** 10% of infants eat and sleep irregularly and are distressed by new experiences; they often form insecure-resistant (Type C) attachments.

You will notice these proportions don't match Ainsworth's observations (she found 70% to be Type B, not 40%). This is because there is an INTERACTION between the child's temperament and the parent's behaviour: sensitive and responsive parents turn many 'slow to warm up' babies into securely attached Type Bs but a few parents neglect their children and these babies turn into resistant Type Cs instead.

> *INTERACTIONISM solves the puzzle of babies learning their attachment style from the way their parents treat them versus babies being born with a temperament that makes them form certain sorts of attachments regardless of their parents' behaviour..*

EFFECT ON DEVELOPMENT OF DAYCARE

You have already studied whether daycare damages development or not: **John Bowlby** warns that it would and **Jay Belsky** repeats this concern (especially for full-time daycare before the child is 12 months old) but **Kathy Sylva** downplays it. The findings from studies can be summarised:

- **Memory**: Children who spent more time in nursery daycare score higher on short-term memory tests; this benefit lasts through primary school.
- **Cognitive development**: High-quality daycare is linked to boosts in scores in tests of Maths, reading and problem-solving.
- **Social skills**: High-quality care is linked to improved **cooperation** and **self control** but this benefit seems to disappear by school age
- **Behaviour problems**: Even high-quality care does not reduce behaviour problems associated with daycare (such as aggression)
- **Conflict**: More time spent in nursery daycare is linked to reports of more conflict with parents and teachers.

A good summary of the conflicting information is from **Helen Bee (1997)**:

The crucial issue is the discrepancy between the level of stimulation that the child would receive at home and the quality of day care. When the day care setting for the child provides more enrichment than the child would normally receive at home, we see some beneficial cognitive effects. When day care is less stimulating than the child's home care would have been, it has negative effects – **Helen Bee**

DAYCARE, TEMPERAMENT & GENDER

Belsky & Pluess (2011) studied the effect of daycare on American children with different temperaments. They studied children when they were pre-5 to identify 'Difficult' temperaments; they studied these children again at 15 to look for signs of EXTERNALISING BEHAVIOUR (which is behaving aggressively or delinquently to express inner unhappiness).

'Difficult' children who experienced low-quality daycare showed more externalising behaviours than children with other temperaments. However, there was no difference between the temperaments when the children experienced high-quality daycare.

The effects of daycare might also vary by gender. **Kottelenberg & Lehrer (2017)** analysed the effects of daycare on 5-year-olds in Quebec, Canada, where the Government subsidises daycare so much it only costs $7 a day.

- **Boys** who suffer negative effects show hyperactivity and poor concentration; they are more likely to be in nursery daycare
- **Girls** who suffer negative effects show emotional anxiety and depression; they are more likely to be in home-based daycare

However, the study points out that the differences may be due to the parents rather than the children: parents tend to withdraw from their girls more than their boys (e.g. they are two times more likely to stop doing special activities with girls once they were in daycare), perhaps viewing these sort of activities as 'someone else's responsibility.'

Possibly boys are more demanding than girls and insist on special activities with their parents – or perhaps parents worry more about their children in nursery than in homecare and feel they have to 'make it up' to them at home.

EFFECTS OF AUTISM ON DEVELOPMENT

You have studied how autism is a DEVELOPMENTAL DISORDER (p43): it is a delay or the complete failure of aspects of normal development taking place. There are some clear developmental warning signs for autism:

- **Language deficit:** children with autism learn language slowly and may prefer single words rather than forming sentences or repeat back what others say; they may not develop intonation in their speak (so they speak flatly, without emotion)

- **Social deficit:** children with autism might not respond to their own name, reject cuddles or react with distress or anger when asked to do things; they might not be aware of personal space, avoid eye contact and prefer to play alone
- **Abnormal behaviour:** autistic children may engage in repetitive movements (rocking, spinning); they may play in a repetitive and unimaginative way; they might have strong food preferences (focusing on shape or colour rather than taste)

EVALUATING NATURE VS NURTURE IN ATTACHMENT AO3

If attachment is entirely down to NURTURE (environment and upbringing), then we can 'fix' children with developmental problems by intervening in their upbringing, such as sending them to high-quality daycare or setting up parenting classes for their families.

If attachment is more a matter of NATURE (genes and temperament), then there's little that can be done to 'fix' developmental problems. Expensive interventions like the UK Sure Start campaign (which provides free daycare for families in need) will be a waste of money – or else will only benefit the sort of children who were going to do well at school anyway.

> *This turns into a political question about the relationship between governments and families. Left-wing politicians (like the UK Labour Party) tend to view child development as largely down to nurture; right-wing politicians (like the UK Conservative Party) tend to view it as more down to nature.*

If we take an INTERACTIONIST view, then things get complicated. Environment and upbringing **do** make a difference to development, but the particular difference they make very much depends on the child itself. This means it becomes very important to TARGET interventions on the right families (something Sure Start is accused of failing to do). In particular, interventions need to target 'Difficult' and 'Slow to Settle' children and also children whose parents are unresponsive or insensitive to their needs.

> *"Insensitive" parents aren't necessarily nasty people. They could just be parents who work long shifts, or who are raising families single-handedly, or who are caring for sick or disabled family members or who have mental health issues themselves.*

Most of the evidence you have studied suggests that the interactionist view is correct: nature and nurture do interact in children's development but it's hard to identify whether genes or environment are more responsible for how a particular child turns out. Two children will respond to different ways to being put in daycare or cared for at home: some will benefit, some will suffer and for others it will make no measurable difference.

REVISING DAYCARE, AUTISM & NATURE-NURTURE

DEFINITIONS

ABA
ADULT ATTACHMENT INTERVIEW
AUTISM
CBT
EMPATHISING
EPPE
ETHNOCENTRISM
EXTREME MALE BRAIN
FOETAL TESTOSTERONE LEVEL
SECCYD
SYSTEMISING
TEMPERAMENT
THEORY OF MIND

RESEARCH SUMMARIES

BARON-COHEN *ET AL.* (1985)
BELSKY (1986)
BELSKY & PLUESS (2011)
BELSKY & ROVINE (1988)
CHAPMAN *Et AL.* (2006)
KANNER (1943)
KOREN-KARIE (2001)
KOTTELENBERG & LEHRER (2017)
SCHAFFER & EMERSON (1964)
SYLVA *ET AL.* (2003)

RESEARCH

Read one of these articles from the Guardian website (**www.theguardian.com**) Add details to your notes

- The great nursery debate (Gentleman, 2010)
- What my son's autism has taught me (Mitchell, 2017)
- Child of the collective (Shpancer, 2011 – growing up on a *kibbutz*)

COMPREHENSION QUESTIONS

1. What are the financial costs of daycare?
2. What is high-quality daycare like?
3. What harm can daycare cause children?
4. What is an interactionist theory of daycare?
5. Why is the daycare debate socially sensitive?
6. What are the main symptoms of autism?
7. What is the biological evidence for the Extreme Male Brain?
8. What is the behavioural evidence for the Extreme Male Brain?
9. How does the Sally-Anne Task work?
10. What's the difference between CBT and ABA as therapies for autism?
11. What is cross-cultural research?
12. What is unusual about childhood in a *kibbutz*?

EXAM-STYLE QUESTIONS

David and Jenny are worried about their son Rex. Although he is 2 years old, Rex does not speak or play with other children. He stacks his building blocks and becomes distressed if they are moved or other toys are offered.

(a) State two features of autism present in the example above. [2 marks AO1]

(b) Explain one strength and one weakness of a non-biological explanation of autism. [4 marks AO3]

(c) Using your knowledge of Psychology, explain and evaluate therapies for autistic children; you must make reference to Rex in your answer. [16 marks AO1+AO2+AO3]

CHILD PSYCHOLOGY: METHODS

What's this topic about?

This introduces you to the main methodologies in Child Psychology, in particular the use of OBSERVATIONS and QUESTIONNAIRE/INTERVIEWS (termed 'self reports'). You will also look again at cross-cultural research from a methods angle, consider data analysis and revisit ethics with a focus on research with child participants.

You will have covered some of these ideas already as part of the AS or Year 1 course and in Unit 2A (Clinical Psychology):

Observations

Observations were introduced as part of Learning Theory: **Bandura** and **Watson & Rayner** both observed children in a controlled setting and your Learning Practical was an observation. Several other studies use the observational method: **Milgram** observed participants in a controlled setting, **Sherif** observed children in a naturalistic setting (a summer camp) and **Raine *et al.*** used brain imaging techniques (PET scans), which are a type of observation. **Rosenhan**'s 'pseudopatient' study was also a naturalistic observation.

Self Reports

Self reports were introduced as part of the Social Approach and your Social Practical was an interview or a survey. **Sherif** used questionnaires to measure the boys' feelings of friendship or hostility towards each other and he carried out unstructured interviews (which he secretly recorded) getting the boys to talk about their relationships. **Freud** based his psychodynamic theory on interviews with patients (including one interview with a 5-year-old boy called 'Little Hans') and **Bandura** used questionnaires to get nursery teachers to rate the aggression of the children in his 'Bobo doll' study.

Cross Cultural Research

Many cross-cultural variations were carried out **of Milgram**'s obedience study, which are summarised by **Thomas Blass (2012)**. The interesting one is **Kilham & Mann (1974)** who found the Australians (especially Australian women) to be incredibly resistant to authority. Cross-cultural variations of **Sherif**'s 'Robbers Cave' study suggest other cultures do not react to inter-group competition the same way as Americans: British boy scouts were very reluctant to get into conflict according to **Tyerman & Spencer (1983)**.

Ethical Guidelines

The **British Psychological Society (BPS)** introduced its ethical guidelines in 1974. The current edition (2018) states that children under age 16 cannot give informed consent to participate in research and should always be treated as at more than minimal risk because of their vulnerability. Studies like **Sherif**, **Bandura** and **Watson & Rayner** would not pass today's ethical standards.

OBSERVATIONS

Observations were introduced in Unit 1 so this section revises the main points about observations then provides applications for Child Psychology.

Observation is...	Meaning	Advantage	Disadvantage
Naturalistic	In a real world setting with everyday behaviour	High in ecological validity	Hard to replicate or gain consent, behaviour might not occur
Structured	In a situation specially set up by the researcher	Easy to replicate and gain consent, behaviour likely to occur	Low in ecological validity
Overt	Participants know they are being observed	Easy to gain consent, convenient to record	Demand characteristics, researcher effects
Covert	Participants don't know they are being observed	Reduces demand characteristics and researcher effects	Hard to gain consent, difficult to record
Non-participant	Researcher is not part of the situation	Easier to remain objective and record things	May lack validity and insight
Participant	Researcher is part of the situation	High in validity, may produce insight	Hard to remain objective and record things
Quantitative	Data is in the form of numbers or tallies	Suitable for statistical analysis, reliable, objective	Reductionist, may lack insight
Tallying	Counting with dashes each time a behaviour occurs	Quick way of recording quantitative data	Can't link particular tally to particular incident later
Qualitative	Data is in the form of words	Rich detail, may produce insight	Not suitable for statistical analysis, unreliable, subjective

The main strength of all observations is that you are recording BEHAVIOUR which is EMPIRICAL EVIDENCE (it's based on the 5 senses). This sort of evidence can be shared with other people:

- you can have INTER-RATER RELIABILITY if you have multiple observers
- you can have TEST-RETEST RELIABILITY if you film behaviour and watch it again

Empirical evidence is important for the SCIENTIFIC STATUS of psychological research. Observing behaviour stands in contrast to studying cognitions (thoughts, feelings) which will always be mysterious since they cannot be observed directly.

Another strength is that observations focus on what participants actually do, rather than what they claim they would do. This VALIDITY is in contrast to using self reports (interviews and questionnaires) which allow respondents to say what they think they would do in situations (but possibly they are mistaken about that).

The main weakness of observations is that behaviour has to be INTERPRETED by the researcher. This means the researcher's own biases influence what they think the behaviour means. This goes as far as deciding what behaviours should even feature in the observation as behavioural categories.

Another weakness is that observations only describe external behaviour, not the thoughts and feelings that lie behind it. For example, Milgram observed participants delivering electric shocks, but couldn't know whether they were taking it seriously.

OBSERVATIONS USED IN CHILD PSYCHOLOGY

Schaffer & Emerson (1964) used observations on 60 babies in their homes (**naturalistic observation**) to record behaviour that suggested stranger and separation anxiety and social referencing. (Schaffer & Emerson also used self reports so this study has MIXED METHODOLOGY).

Ainsworth & Wittig (1969) created the **Strange Situation Procedure (SSP)** which is a **structured observation** that measures separation anxiety, stranger anxiety and reunion behaviour. The SSP was also used by **Belsky & Rovine (1988)**.

The case study of Genie by **Curtiss (1977)** and the studies of institutionalised children by **Robertson (1953)** and **Spitz (1946)** all use **naturalistic observations** (with Robertson filming his observation). The study of Genie also involved **structured observation** (setting tasks for Genie) and could be viewed as a **participant observation** because as well as studying Genie the researchers were also her carers while the project lasted.

Finally, although it doesn't involve human children, **Harlow (1958)** observed the behaviour of rhesus monkeys in a **structured** setting (the wire and cloth mothers).

EVALUATING OBSERVATIONAL METHODS IN CHILD PSYCHOLOGY AO3

Shaffer & Emerson (1965) observed real babies, in their own homes surrounded by their own family. This is a good example of high ecological validity producing natural behaviour in the participants. The same could be said of **Robertson (1953)** and **Spitz (1946)** observing real child patients in real hospitals. This can be contrasted with **Ainsworth's SSP** which places infants in unfamiliar locations and puts them in the company of strangers.

However, the difference might not be that significant. Just introducing researchers into a family home or a hospital ward makes the other adults there behave differently and children probably sense the change and react to it. These naturalistic observations might not really be that natural.

On the other hand, the structured situations used by **Ainsworth** allow for the research to be replicated and rule out EXTRANEOUS VARIABLES. For example, the homes that **Shaffer & Emerson** visited could have had other things going on (birthday parties, money worries, noisy neighbours or naughty siblings) that interfered with the observation; none of this affects the results of the SSP. Similarly, although **Harlow**'s monkey experiments were artificial, they were replicable and had no outside variables interfering.

Robertson filmed Laura's stay in hospital and this means his observation is reliable as it can viewed by other observers. However, Laura was in hospital for 8 days and Robertson's film only lasts 45 minutes, so Robertson clearly 'cherry-picked' footage that supported his theory that children are emotionally damaged by separation from their caregivers.

The SSP uses one-way mirrors to observe the children covertly. It's not clear how important this is. Do children notice or care if they are being observed? It might be that all observations of young infants are effectively 'covert' since the child doesn't understand what is going on. However, the one-way mirror ensures that the child is definitely reacting to the arrival of the stranger, not to the researchers.

What all of these studies have in common is that they draw conclusions from the behaviour of children, not what the children claim they are feeing (which could be 'putting a brave face on it') or what the parents think they are feeling (which might be distorted by a need to present themselves as good parents or an unwillingness to admit their children are distressed).

Several of these studies used a MIXED METHODOLOGY, combining self reports with observations: **Shaffer & Emerson** interviewed the parents about their child's behaviour and asked the mothers to write diaries; **Belsky & Rovine** also interviewed the families about daycare. This makes it less likely the researchers will misinterpret the child's behaviour, reading things into it that aren't there.

INTERVIEWS & QUESTIONNAIRES

Self reports (interviews & questionnaires) were introduced in Unit 1 so this section revises the main points then provides applications for Child Psychology.

Self report is...	Meaning	Advantage	Disadvantage
Questionnaire	Using written questions to gather data	Replicable, fast and cheap for big sample sizes	Requires respondent is literate, questions may be misread or ignored
Psychometric test	A questionnaire that produces a score for a mental trait (e.g. IQ)	Produces quantitative data for statistical analysis	Reductionist: reduces complex mental traits to numbers
Interview	Using spoken questions to gather data	Encourages honesty, allows for socially sensitive topics	Unreliable, slow and expensive for large sample sizes
Structured interview	The questions are fixed in advance and asked in the same order	Replicable, doesn't require training, results can be compared	Cannot correct mistakes or follow up interesting answers, may feel unnatural
Semi-structured interview	Some questions are fixed in advance but others are improvised	Replicable but interviewer can correct mistakes or follow up answers	Somewhat unreliable, requires trained interviewers to carry it out
Unstructured interview	All the questions are improvised	More like a natural conversation, encourages trust & honesty	Unreliable, hard to compare results since no two interviews are alike
Open questions	Questions the respondent can answer in their own words	Valid answers, reveals respondents'' own thoughts	Unreliable since respondents may answer in different ways or lengths
Closed questions	Questions where the respondent chooses answers from a list	Reliable, can create quantitative data for analysis	Invalid since list might not include answer respondent wants to give (FORCED CHOICE)
Quantitative	Data is in the form of numbers or tallies	Suitable for statistical analysis, reliable, objective	Reductionist, may lack insight into real thoughts
Qualitative	Data is in the form of words	Rich detail, may produce insight into real thoughts	Not suitable for statistical analysis, unreliable, subjective

The main strength of all self reports is that you are recording MENTAL STATES OR TRAITS which cannot be directly observed. Knowing people's beliefs and intentions helps researchers interpret their behaviour.

Another strength is that self reports enable respondents to contradict or correct the researcher's assumptions, sometimes expressing surprising ideas or perceptions. This is in contrast to observations, where biased researchers can interpret any behaviour in line with their theory.

A weakness of self-reports is that they do not generate EMPIRICAL EVIDENCE which is important for a truly scientific theory. Empirical evidence is important for the SCIENTIFIC STATUS of psychological research. Reporting thoughts and feelings stands in contrast to directly observing behaviour; this can be replicated and shared.

Another weakness is that self reports often focus on what participants think they would do, rather than what they actually do. This lack of VALIDITY is in contrast to observations, which study actual behaviour.

SELF REPORTS USED IN CHILD PSYCHOLOGY

Freud (1909) used interviews with his patients, notably his case study of 5-year-old 'Little Hans' who suffered developmental problems (a crippling phobia of horses) which Freud believed was caused by the boy's unconscious hatred of his father.

Bowlby (1944) also used interviews with his juvenile thieves and their families; the boys also completed **psychometric tests** to measure their mental states.

Most of the big **longitudinal studies** into daycare (e.g. **SECCYD** and **EPPE**) use **psychometric tests** to measure whether the children are improving in their cognitive skills or developing emotional problems; they also get day carers and parents to complete normal questionnaires on the child's behaviour. **Belsky & Rovine (1989)** interviewed parents about the effects of daycare and 98% of the parents of children in the EPPE were interviewed about their home environment.

Koren-Karie (2001) used an interview technique called the **Adult Attachment Interview (AAI)** which is a **semi-structured interview** for measuring how attached adults are to their parents and children. It has 20 fixed questions, takes about an hour to work through and places the respondent in one of four categories of attachment. The AAI also features in the **contemporary study** by **Cassibba et al. (2013)**.

Finally, **Simon Baron-Cohen** has created or co-created many **psychometric tests** to identify cognitive deficits in autism, such as the **'Eyes in the Mind' Test**, the **Empathy Quotient Scale (EQS)** and the **Sally-Anne Test**.

EVALUATING SELF REPORT METHODS IN CHILD PSYCHOLOGY AO3

Obviously, very young infants cannot be interviewed and even children of age 2+ present problems for interviewers (small vocabulary, low attention span and a tendency towards **demand characteristics**).

> *Remember, demand characteristics are when a respondent answers based on what they think the researcher's aims are. They don't have to guess RIGHT about that. Most children have very little idea about what psychologists are trying to do, but they do like to please adults.*

Freud and **Bowlby** both interviewed their participants. Because these interviews are face-to-face they also include elements of **observation** too. The difference is that Freud's interviews were entirely **unstructured** (because, in order to explore unconscious motivations, Freud had to follow his intuitions and feelings) whereas Bowlby aimed to be more SCIENTIFIC and carried out **semi-structured interviews** along with **psychometric tests**.

This is part of a general turn away from Freud's approach in favour of a more **scientific approach** to Psychology in the 20th century. At the time, Bowlby was heavily criticised by Freud's influential followers for rejecting Freudian methods and ideas. However, by the 1980s, Freud's ideas had been removed from the DSM-III and replaced by scientific approaches. The use of psychometric tests in the **SECCYD** and **EPPE** projects are further attempts to bring scientific status to research into childhood.

When Bowlby was at work, the idea that children experience deep distress and lasting damage from separation was novel and not widely accepted. This is a good example of using self reports to expose **hidden mental states** and experiences that **contradict ordinary assumptions**.

A similar benefit of self reports can be seen in the research into **autism**, which uses ingenious psychometric tests to show that autistic children are not 'retarded' but instead suffer from a very different form of cognitive deficit that had not been noticed before.

Despite this, self reports to not provide empirical evidence of mental states: the respondents can answer falsely or be mistaken. This is one of the reasons why there is still debate about **daycare**, despite the huge amount of research carried out into it. Critics argue that IQ tests are not valid indicators of a child's ability, particularly children from working class, non-white or non-English-speaking backgrounds. They simply measure whether children are good at passing tests.

Despite this, self reports can be improved by using MIXED METHODOLOGY (such as **Belsky & Rovine** using interviews and observations). The AIS used by **Koren-Karie** produces results that successfully predict the SSP observation on children, which suggests it is both valid (i.e. it tells the truth) and reliable (i.e. it is consistent).

SAMPLING

Sampling introduced in Unit 1 so this section revises the main points then provides applications for Child Psychology.

Sample is...	Meaning	Advantage	Disadvantage
Opportunity	Choosing participants who are convenient (available at the time)	Easy, quick, inexpensive	Experimenter bias by choosing unrepresentative participants
Random	Choosing participants in an unbiased way (e.g. names from a hat)	No bias	Requires list of all possible participants; random selection can still be unrepresentative
Self-selecting (volunteer)	Advertising then choosing any participants who respond	No experimenter bias	Time consuming, participant bias as people who respond may be unrepresentative
Stratified	Opportunity or volunteer sample including numbers of people in different categories (strata)	Will be representative of the strata used	Time consuming, choice of strata may be biased (e.g. researcher might miss out important strata like race)

Samples are representative if they contain the same mix of people that are found in the TARGET POPULATION. Samples tend to be unrepresentative if the selection was BIASED (the research didn't include important people for personal reasons) or if it contains too many ANOMALIES (unusual people who will SKEW the results).

- Making a sample larger does NOT make it more representative
- However, large samples may contain fewer ANOMALIES who would skew the results of a small sample

The best way to make a sample representative is to STRATIFY it (making sure you contain the same proportion of men, women, different ethnicities, rich and poor, ages, etc. that are found in the target population). However, it's not always obvious which strata are important and which are not. For example, many early Psychology studies (like **Milgram**) didn't include women or (like **Sherif**) ethnic minorities.

Do you think star sign (e.g. Gemini, Virgo and Scorpio) is an important strata? Should Child Psychology studies make sure that 1/12th of the sample is from each sign of the Zodiac? Most Psychologists don't think so – but maybe they're wrong!

If you sample this tasty sauce, you might get a bit with a chilli in it and think it's hotter than it really is. That would be an anomaly skewing your data. If you take a really BIG sample, a single chilli won't spoil it

SAMPLING USED IN CHILD PSYCHOLOGY

The older studies tend to use small opportunity samples. **Freud (1909)** used his own patients in Vienna and **Bowlby (1944)** used the children who were already clients at his London Clinic in the 1930s. **Shaffer & Emerson (1964)** recruited 64 Glasgow families who were registered with the Infant Welfare Clinic (so also an opportunity sample).

Ainsworth (1967) used 28 babies from the villages in Uganda where she was studying breastfeeding; later **Ainsworth & Bell (1972)** used a much larger sample of 56 American babies and this was recruited through the parents volunteering.

You often read that Ainsworth tested "100 American babies" with the SSP but I can't pin down this number to any particular study. Since she carried out a lot of research at John Hopkins University in the 1970s, they perhaps added up to 100. The number is so often cited that I think candidates could describe Ainsworth's American sample as "100" in the Exam.

Baron-Cohen has tended to sample participants with autism from his Clinic in Cambridge (**opportunity sample**) but he also recruits large **volunteer samples** for his psychometric tests online. For example, Baron-Cohen *et al.* (2014) used data from 811 autistic adults and 3906 healthy controls who completed tests online.

The big longitudinal studies (**SECCYD** and **EPPE**) recruit from day centres and other child carers who volunteer to take part. However, the precise children being used are then **randomly selected** from within each daycentre. The EPPE Project was advertised in 6 different regions to include cities, suburbs, rural villages, rich and poor areas and ethnic diversity, so this is a **stratified sample** of 3000 children. The SECCYD recruited 1200 children in the same way from 10 areas of the USA.

Robertson also used **random sampling**, because the 2-year-old girl Laura was randomly selected from children in the hospital ward to be the subject of Robertson's film.

EVALUATING SAMPLING METHODS IN CHILD PSYCHOLOGY AO3

The problem with **opportunity samples** is that they can reflect the researcher's biases. **Freud**'s patients were chosen by him precisely because their odd symptoms suggested sexual anxiety and **Bowlby** selected his most disturbed young clients to fit in with his theory of maternal deprivation. Bowlby himself admitted that his sample suffered from not including healthy children.

Robertson's use of random sampling is in contrast to the possible bias in Bowlby and Freud: Robertson didn't choose Laura for any qualities that marked her out. Every child in the hospital ward had an equal chance of being picked.

However, it also shows the problem with random sampling. Just because Laura was picked at random, it doesn't mean she was the most representative child on the ward. She could have been unusually emotional or above-averagely tough.

There is a tendency for these researchers like **Ainsworth** to focus on middle class families who are willing to **volunteer** for university-run projects (since they're probably graduates themselves, middle class parents aren't troubled by psychology professors running strange tests on their babies).

Shaffer & Emerson's Glasgow babies are an exception to this trend, since they were able to recruit working class families who agreed to take part when approached by a health visitor. **Bowlby** also studied largely working class children.

Social class matters because there is a strong stereotype that working class families are more warm and affectionate towards their families and middle class families are restrained and worried about 'spoiling' the child. This stereotype lies behind the early view that **autism** was a result of 'cold parenting'.

That's why the **SECCYD** and **EPPE** longitudinal studies are an important step forward, since they go out of their way to recruit large, diverse samples in an unbiased way. However, even these samples are not **statistically stratified**: the researchers took the trouble to make sure the sample was diverse (i.e. including ethnic minorities and different social classes) but didn't make sure the strata matched up precisely to the proportions of such groups in society. For example, 9% of the UK population was non-white according to the 2001 Census, but the EPPE Project didn't make sure that exactly 9% (270) of its participating children were non-white. The researchers in the EPPE Project also admit that some ethnic groups (like Gypsies) were not represented properly in the study.

Baron-Cohen's use of the Internet to recruit large volunteer samples is controversial. On the one hand, many people with autism are more comfortable participating in research studies remotely. On the other hand, you cannot be sure exactly who is taking the test or under what conditions (tired, distracted, drunk). Nevertheless, Baron-Cohen praises the "*statistical power*" of this size of sample which reduces anomalies.

Sampling links to the issue of SOCIAL SENSITIVITY. This is because, if research is dominated by white, middle-class participants, then conclusions about *their* child-rearing practices will be presented as UNIVERSAL (applying to everyone). Social policy might be formed on this basis and working class or ethnic minority parents who have different ways of raising their children could be classed as 'bad parents' and might even be forced to conform to the norms established by biased research.

REVISING OBSERVATIONS, SELF REPORTS & SAMPLES

DEFINITIONS
COVERT OBSERVATION
NATURALISTIC OBSERVATION
OPPORTUNITY SAMPLE
PSYCHOMETRIC TEST
QUALITATIVE DATA
QUANTITATIVE DATA
RANDOM SAMPLE
SEMI-STRUCTURED INTERVIEW
STRATIFIED SAMPLE
STRUCTURED OBSERVATION
TALLYING
VOLUNTEER SAMPLE

PROVIDE RESEARCH EXAMPLES OF:
COVERT OBSERVATION
NATURALISTIC OBSERVATION
OPPORTUNITY SAMPLING
PSYCHOMETRIC TESTING
RANDOM SAMPLING
SEMI-STRUCTURED INTERVIEW
STRUCTURED OBSERVATION
VOLUNTEER SAMPLING

RESEARCH
Take one of these psychometric tests yourself (you can find them online) and evaluate the test

- The Empathy Quotient Scale (EQS) at psychology-tools.com
- The Eyes in the Mind Test at socialintelligence.labinthewild. org
- Relationship Attachment Style Test at testyourself.psychtests.com

COMPREHENSION QUESTIONS
1. How could you carry out a participant observation in a daycare centre?
2. How can demand characteristics be reduced in observations?
3. What is inter-rater reliability?
4. What is empirical evidence?
5. What is an advantage of using a mixed methodology?
6. What is the advantage of asking open questions?
7. What is wrong with small sample sizes?
8. How can bias be reduced in sampling?
9. How can samples be made more representative?
10. What are the problems with sampling online?
11. Why were NICHD and EPPE not *strictly speaking* stratified samples?

EXAM-STYLE QUESTIONS

Luiza wants to know if some children are more insecurely attached than others. She carries out an observation of 2-year-old children at a daycare centre. She times how long it took children to settle and become calm after their parent leaves them.

(a) State the meaning of naturalistic non-participant observation. [2 marks AO1]

(b) Explain how Luiza could investigate the same research question with a questionnaire or interview. [4 marks AO2]

(c) Explain and evaluate the use of naturalistic observations in child psychology; you must make reference to Luiza in your answer. [16 marks AO1+AO2+AO3]

CROSS-CULTURAL RESEARCH

Cultural differences were introduced in Unit 1 and explored in Unit 2A (Clinical Psychology) with the idea of cross-cultural research, which is research that sets out to compare one cultural group with another. A good example is the **classic study** by **Van Ijzendoorn & Kroonenberg (1988**, p87**)**.

The pioneer of cross-cultural Child Psychology was **Mary Ainsworth** (p30), who explored whether Bowlby's ideas about the mother-child bond were UNIVERSAL (applying to all humans everywhere).

AINSWORTH'S UGANDA STUDIES (AINSWORTH, 1967)

Ainsworth studied 26 breastfeeding mothers in Uganda in the 1960s She visited the families in their homes, about 10 times each over, several months. She carried out **semi-structured interviews** with the mothers (through an interpreter) and **naturalistic observations** of the children (Ainsworth hadn't yet developed her **Strange Situation Procedure**).

Ainsworth found that most of the children were securely attached and used their mothers as a 'safe base' to explore the world around them. She also identified insecurely attached babies who were cried more and were anxious and babies who seemed to be unattached to their mothers. Ainsworth also noticed that this seemed to be linked to the amount of interest the mother took in the baby.

Ugandan mother (photo by: Issa Ahmed Khamis)

AINSWORTH'S AMERICAN STUDIES (AINSWORTH & BELL, 1972)

When Ainsworth moved to the USA, she was able to compare the results of her Uganda research to very different families living in Baltimore, a big US city. Ainsworth recruited 26 middle class families to take part: all had just one child and the mother was a full-time homemaker.

Once again, Ainsworth carried out **naturalistic observations** and **semi-structured interviews** in the homes. However, this time she also brought the families to John Hopkins University to take part in her **Strange Situation Procedure (SSP**, p32**)**, a **structured observation**.

Ainsworth found similar results to Uganda, with secure children belonging to responsive mothers and using their mothers as a 'secure base' but insecure children belonging to the less responsive mothers. Ainsworth concludes that these attachment styles are UNIVERSAL.

NATURE VS NURTURE IN ATTACHMENT

Ainsworth's standardised procedures are easy to replicate so her research has been carried on by other psychologists in other cultures:

- **Grossman *et al.* (1985)** studied German families who encourage children to be independent and not to be 'clingy': **insecure-avoidant attachment (Type A)** was more common than in the USA
- **Sagi *et al.* (1985)** studied children on an Israeli *kibbutz* and found more **insecure-resistant attachments (Type C)** than in the USA (perhaps because of lack of exposure to strangers)
- **Miyake *et al.* (1985)** studied Japanese families where the baby is kept close to the mother and not encouraged to explore; **insecure-resistant attachment (Type C)** was more common than in the USA (again, due to lack of exposure to strangers)

These studies are part of the meta-analyses by **Van Ijzendoorn & Kroonenberg** (*c.f.* p87).

This suggests there are broad similarities but also differences in attachment between cultures. **Mi Kyoung Jin (2012)** suggests these conclusions:

1. It is UNIVERSAL for children to form attachments
2. Secure attachment is the NORM (the most common) in every culture
3. Secure attachment is formed by sensitive nurture (the SENSITIVE CAREGIVER HYPOTHESIS)
4. Secure attachment leads to the later DEVELOPMENT of social skills and emotional health

This is a combination of NATURE and NURTURE because:

- It is NATURAL to form secure attachments, but
- NURTURE influences whether the attachment is secure or insecure

META-ANALYSES IN CROSS CULTURAL RESEARCH

Meta-analyses are also called **'review studies'**. They do not generate new data or original research; instead they gather together previous research and draw overall conclusions from that. Meta-analyses often have to develop new statistical approaches because the original studies that are being compared often have different scoring systems and probably different definitions and concepts, so comparing them isn't always easy.

A famous meta-analysis is **Van Ijzendoorn & Kroonenberg (1988**, p87**)** who compared al the versions of the SSP that had been carried out in different countries up to that point. The contemporary studies by **Cassibba *et al.* (2013**, p90**)** and **Li *et al.* (2013**, p96**)** are also meta-analyses.

EVALUATING CROSS CULTURAL RESEARCH AO3

The biggest problem for traditional research into attachment is ETHNOCENTRISM. This is a form of bias that regards your own culture as normal or natural. Most of the early leaders in Psychology were educated, middle class, white males:

- There is a tendency to view women as 'natural caregivers' and the maternal bond as more important than bonds with fathers or daycarers (**Bowlby** tends to do this)
- There is a tendency to view the 'nuclear family' of mother and father with their own children as normal and natural (**Freud** tends to do this)
- There is a tendency to regard middle class parenting styles as the most important to understand. Some psychologists seem to view these as particularly good (e.g. **Ainsworth**) but others seem to see them as problematic (e.g. **Kanner** and **Bettelheim** on autism).
- There is an assumption that whatever is true for families in Europe or America will be true for all families everywhere

Cross-cultural research challenges ethnocentrism, revealing which experiences really are UNIVERSAL (true for all humans everywhere) and which are local customs. For example, **Bowlby** just assumes that maternal deprivation is a problem for all children, but **Ainsworth** tests this in Uganda and finds that children do in fact behave similarly there.

Other critics have debated whether the SSP itself is an ethnocentric tool for studying attachment. The argument is that putting a child alone in an unfamiliar place to be confronted by a complete stranger is something that would simply never happen in Japanese society or in an Israeli *kibbutz*. Therefore these children will act unnaturally during the SSP and you can't draw conclusions about them or their culture from this.

Another criticism is that cultures differ in lots of ways when it comes to childhood and parenting: they treat children differently and have different expectations of children. Something like the SSP is simply too REDUCTIONIST to study cultural differences because it leaves out everything that makes a culture distinctive.

Heather Montgomery (2013) provides some examples of these cultural differences in childhood:

- **Beng** (West African) parents view children as visitors from the spirit world and often treat them with religious respect
- **Fulani** (also West African) parents view children as workers and start giving them chores at age 4 and proper work (e.g. making and selling food) by age 6
- **Inuit** (Canadian native peoples) parents are very tolerant of children, because they view them as irrational
- **Yanomami** (Amazon native people): girls help in the home at a young age and run a household by age 10, marrying and having babies by 13; boys play into their teens and marry later

Yanomami children from Venezuela (photo: Ambar)

Meta-analyses are often used to draw similarities and differences across cultures. The availability of research on Internet libraries makes it easier to search for studies than in the past. However, a problem with meta-analyses is the FILE DRAWER PROBLEM. Because studies only tend to get published if they find something statistically significant, meta-analyses can be skewed in favour of differences because studies that didn't find a difference don't make it into the review. A solution is to include unpublished research (like student dissertations) but since unpublished work hasn't been PEER-REVIEWED this will lower the SCIENTIFIC STATUS of the review.

LONGITUDINAL STUDIES

Longitudinal design was introduced in Unit 2A (Clinical Psychology) so this section revises the main points then provides applications for Child Psychology. A longitudinal study looks at how a group of participants (a COHORT) change over time.

Study is...	Meaning	Advantage	Disadvantage
Prospective	Studying a cohort of participants who develop over time	Reveals trends and changes over time	Sample attrition (participants dropping out), time & expense
Retrospective	Studying the past background of a cohort of participants	Reveals common causes or factors behind the present	Records may be lacking or incomplete, memories may be faulty (e.g. schemas)
Cross-sectional	Comparing different cohorts of participants from different points in time	No sample attrition; quick & cheaper; reveals trends and changes over time	Not comparing like with like (low validity); extraneous variables may make cohorts differ

PROSPECTIVE studies are what most people think of as 'longitudinal'. Researchers select a cohort (such as children all born at the same time) then revisit them at regular intervals (such as monthly or yearly) and record how they change. This is similar to REPEATED MEASURES DESIGN in experiments because the same participants are used each time.

RETROSPECTIVE studies select a cohort that all share a similar condition (such as autism) then looks **backward** in time to examine their past history and look for factors they share in common that might explain their condition.

CROSS-SECTIONAL studies are an alternative to longitudinal design. Researchers get several different cohorts who are all at different points in time or different stages in development then compare them on tests. This is similar to INDEPENDENT GROUPS DESIGN in experiments because different participants are used in each condition.

LONGITUDINAL DESIGN USED IN CHILD PSYCHOLOGY

Shaffer & Emerson (1964) uses a **prospective longitudinal design**. They focus on 60 Glasgow babies who were all 2-6 months old when first studied. This cohort was studied until they were 18 months old. The researchers record how the babies changed in their responses to their parents, other family members and to strangers.

Bowlby (1944) uses a **retrospective longitudinal design**. He focuses on 44 'juvenile thieves' and investigates their past history (specifically their separation from their mothers) to work out how their background differed from the non-delinquent Controls.

Curtiss (1977) uses both types of longitudinal design: the study is **prospective** because it follows Genie over 4 years, recording her language and social development; it is **retrospective** because it also looks into Genie's abused childhood as an explanation for her condition.

The **SECCYD** and **EPPE** projects are **prospective longitudinal studies** that take 1200 (SECCYD) and 3000 (EPPE) children in daycare and follow them through to school age. However, the EPPE Project is also **cross-sectional** because it also looks at children of who start at different ages (from 3 to 11) and compares them with each other.

> *The main idea of a cross-sectional study is that if you look at a 3-year-old and a 11-year-old you can ASSUME that the 3-year-old will develop into the 11-year-old, whereas a prospective study actually waits and watches that change happen.*

EVALUATING LONGITUDINAL DESIGN IN CHILD PSYCHOLOGY AO3

If you just studied a child on one occasion (a SNAPSHOT STUDY) then its behaviour could be due to its mood that day rather than revealing anything significant about attachment. By returning to view the child again and again, **prospective studies** like **Shaffer & Emerson** show the underlying development going on.

Similarly, a snapshot of a child's test performance could be explained by distractions or poor teaching, but prospective studies like **SECCYD** and **EPPE** show children's scores changing in systematic ways as they grow up.

SAMPLE ATTRITION is a problem because the sample size gets smaller the longer the study lasts, with participants dropping out. Moreover, the children who leave the study tend to be the most interesting ones (from a psychological point of view): they are the ones who get expelled from schools, truant, go to prison, become homeless or get hospitalised as well as those who move away.

Sometimes it's hard to assemble a cohort for a prospective study. For example, **Bowlby** had to use a **retrospective design** because he couldn't know in advance which children wee going to suffer from **maternal deprivation**. He had to identify children who had *already* experienced separation by investigating their pasts.

Cross-sectional designs solve the problems of longitudinal studies: they are cheap and quick and there's no danger of sample attrition. However, a cross-sectional design really just compares different snapshot studies of different children at different ages. **EPPE** found that children raised in daycare were more aggressive at age 6 but this had lessened at age 11, but they were *looking at different children*. It's possible the 11-year-olds weren't aggressive either at 6 and that the 6-year-olds weren't going to grow out of it given time.

THE ETHICS OF RESEARCHING WITH CHILDREN

You were introduced to ethical guidelines for researchers as part of Unit 1. The **BPS Code of Ethics (2018)** emphasises **respect**, **competence**, **responsibility** and **integrity**. These principles are put into practice in the following ways:

Guideline is...	Meaning	Advantage	Disadvantage
Consent	Participants must make an INFORMED CHOICE to take part	Informed participants understand what will happen to them	It's not possible to inform children or some people with autism if they lack language or self-awareness
Deception	Participants must not be misled by researchers	Honest researchers can be trusted and establish a good reputation	It may be necessary to deceive participants to avoid DEMAND CHARACTERISTICS
Withdrawal	Participants must be able to leave a study (or have their data deleted) without justifying why	Withdrawing participants have AUTONOMY and are protecting themselves	Children and some people with autism may lack the language or social skills to withdraw
Protection	Participants must not be harmed and must leave in the same state they entered	This shows RESPECT for unharmed participants and establishes a good reputation	Some research will always be stressful for participants but stress does not have to lead to permanent damage
Confidentiality	The identities of participants should be kept secret	Protects participants from association with SOCIALLY SENSITIVE issues	Some participants generate intense media interest (e.g. Genie) or would shed more light if identified (e.g. Little Albert)
Debriefing	All the details of the study should be explained at the end	This can make up for necessary deception (up to a point)	It's not possible to debrief young children or severely autistic participants
Competence	Researchers must not make or imply claims they are not qualified to do (e.g. diagnosis)	Prevents alarming parents by suggesting their children have a disability	Parents may assume researchers are competent (e.g. as doctors or psychiatrists) even though they don't claim to be

BPS Guidelines make it clear that children under age 16 cannot give informed consent and are especially at risk in psychological studies. However, parents or guardians can give PRESUMPTIVE CONSENT (consenting *on behalf of* the child).

) NATIONS CONVENTION ON THE RIGHTS OF THE CHILD (UNCRC, ₋₋₋)

The UNCRC is an international agreement on children's rights which became part of UK law in 1992 (it has not been ratified by the USA, but America has its own body of rights). The UNCRC defines as child as anyone under the age of 18 (rather than 16, so this is more demanding than BPS Guidelines). It is based on 4 Principles:

The 4 Ps	Meaning	Advantage	Disadvantage
Participation	Children have the right to be researched and their views taken seriously	Children (or children from certain backgrounds) cannot be excluded from studies	Conflicts with PROTECTION since children can be excluded from studies if their parents don't consent
Protection	Children must be kept safe from harm, including activities which harm their development	Children are especially vulnerable and may suffer long-term effects of research	Protecting children may deprive them of right to PARTICIPATION; not all effects of research can be foreseen
Provision	Children should be provided with all the services they need to flourish	Research should not deprive children of things to see how they respond to deprivation	Deprivation needs to be studied and so does low-quality daycare or unresponsive parenting
Privacy	Children's identities should be kept secret and their home life left unchanged by research	This helps PROTECT children from the longer-term consequences of research	SOCIALLY SENSITIVE research does need to investigate family life too

These Principles resemble the BPS Ethical Guidelines, but in many ways they are strengthened and proceed from the basis of the needs of the child rather than the intentions of the researcher.

> *The UNCRC wasn't designed primarily for guiding psychological research: it is supposed to cover child labour, child refugees, children in war, child sex abuse and national laws.*

APPLYING UNCRC TO CHILD PSYCHOLOGY

Many of the studies in this topic were carried out before the UNCR or even before the BPS Ethical Guidelines (e.g. **Bowlby, Robertson, Shaffer & Emerson**, most of **Ainsworth**'s research). American studies like the **SECCYD** are not covered by the UNCRC.

The main study that has been influenced by the UNCRC is the **EPPE Project** which was conducted in the late 1990s and early 2000s in the UK.

EVALUATING THE UNCRC FOR CHILD PSYCHOLOGY AO3

The BPS Guidelines are written specifically for psychologists. They come from the perspective that it is good and necessary that psychological research is carried out and that some of it needs to be carried out on children (or has implications for them even if they aren't the main participants, e.g. research into mothers' responses to their babies).

This means that the BPS Guidelines have a practical position: they are about MAXIMISING BENEFITS and MINIMISING HARM and this is done through RISK ASSESSMENT. The BPS takes it for granted that children in research may suffer *some* distress, but that an ethical psychologist will minimise this and occasion it only when necessary for socially beneficial research.

The UNCRC is much more stringent. It was written from the perspective of the child's dignity and human rights. These can't be compromised 'for the sake of science'. Societies in the past have tended to view children as passive and even expendable, but the UNCRC aims to change all that and challenge the fundamental way we view children.

This means the UNCRC can be very restrictive for Child Psychologists. The **Strange Situation Procedure (SSP)** deliberately creates distress for children by depriving them of their mother and introducing a scary stranger: this would go against the baby's rights to both **protection** and **provision**. Bowlby's labelling of his participants as "juvenile thieves" is disrespectful of their participation too.

Even the **EPPE Project** has problems: the lengthy home-based interviews invade the child's right to **privacy** while the (unintended) exclusion of Gypsy and other 'traveller' children violate their right to **participation**.

Ultimately, the UNCRC is more of an aim or goal than a set of rules. The UN won't arrest psychologists who breach its standards, whereas the BPS *will* suspend psychologists who ignore its Guidelines (which will definitely ruin their career).

There are two perspectives on the UNCRC:

1. It is an aspirational document that raises awareness of children's rights and encourages psychologists to 'raise their game' in how they treat children. Recent editions of the BPS Guidelines have been brought into line with the UNCRC and, as a result, psychologists today are far more considerate and respectful of children than they were in the past.
2. It is a restrictive document that has a 'chilling effect' on psychological research by putting the rights of children above their own long-term welfare and the good of the society they live in (e.g. getting to the bottom of the 'Daycare Debate'). Important research from the past would not be possible today under these restrictions.

REVISING CULTURE, LONGITUDINAL DESIGN & ETHICS

DEFINITIONS
COHORT
CROSS-SECTIONAL STUDY
DEBRIEFING
META-ANALYSIS
PRESUMPTIVE CONSENT
PROSPECTIVE STUDY
RETROSPECTIVE STUDY
UNCRC
UNIVERSAL

RESEARCH SUMMARIES
AINSWORTH (1967)
AINSWORTH & BELL (1972)
GROSSMAN *ET AL.* (1985)
MIYAKE *ET AL.* (1985)
SAGI *Et AL.* (1985)

RESEARCH
Find out more about childhood in a non-Western culture, such as:
- Child labour or child soldiers
- The Ik people of Uganda who abandon their children at age 3
- Street children in cities like Rio
- Why Dutch children are the happiest in the world
- *How Cultures Around the World Think About Parenting* (Choi, 2014 on ideas.ted.com)
- *Children in England near bottom of international happiness table* (Gayle, 2016 at theguardian.com)
- *10 unusual parenting styles from around the world* (Faujour, 2015 at globalcitizen.org)

COMPREHENSION QUESTIONS
1. What did Ainsworth learn from her Uganda studies?
2. What are the universal norms in attachment?
3. What are the cultural differences in attachment?
4. Why are children who grow up in Japan more likely to have Type C attachment?
5. What is the advantage of longitudinal studies?
6. Why is sample attrition a problem?
7. What is the problem with cross-sectional studies?
8. How can samples be made more representative?
9. What are the problems with sampling online?
10. What are the 4 Ps?
11. Why does the UNCRC have a 'chilling effect' on research?

EXAM-STYLE QUESTIONS

The United Nations Convention on the Rights of the Child (UNCRC, 1989) has been signed by almost all the countries in the world and guarantees the safety and dignity of children. It needs to be observed by psychologists studying children in all cultures.

(a) State two examples of cultural differences in child development. [2 marks AO1]

(b) Explain how the UNCRC (1989) affects research into Child Psychology. [4 marks AO2]

(c) Evaluate longitudinal design in child psychology. [8 marks AO1+AO3]

DATA ANALYSIS

Data analysis was introduced in Unit 1 and developed in Unit 2A (Clinical Psychology). The main points will be revised here but only **Grounded Theory (GT)** will be considered from the perspective of Child Psychology.

Quantitative data is...	Meaning	Advantage	Disadvantage
Measures of central tendency	The different types of 'averages' (mean, median and mode)		
Mean	Add up all the values and divide by the size of the set	Useful with interval/ratio level data	May be a value that isn't actually in the set; may be distorted by outliers
Median	The central value when the set is arranged in rank order	Useful with ordinal level data	Doesn't reflect outliers; no actual median if the set is even-numbered
Mode	Most frequent value in the set	Useful with nominal level data	May be several modes or none
Measures of dispersion	Scores showing how the set is spread out (range, standard deviation)		
Range	Highest score minus lowest score	Shows whether there are outliers	Doesn't show how many outliers there are
Standard deviation	Deduct the mean from each score, square the result, divide the sum by the size of the set minus 1, take the square root	Shows how far away from the mean a score has to be to count as unusual	Only useful if there is a mean (interval/ratio level data)

The Specification also singles out FREQUENCY TABLES. These are charts that show how often behaviours occur as a column of varying heights. Unlike a simple bar chart, *the columns are touching*. The **mode** will appear on a frequency table as the highest column(s).

This frequency table shows the frequency of letters appearing in English words. Can you spot the mode (the letter that appears most frequently in words)?

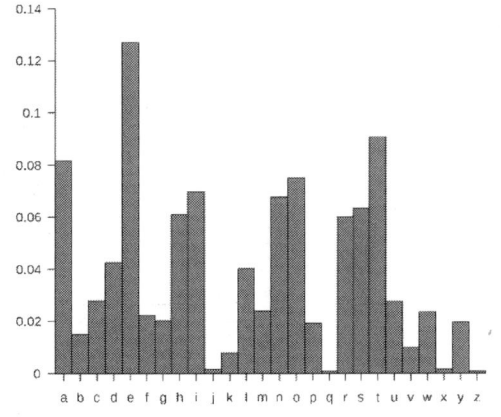

Statistics are...	Meaning	Advantage	Disadvantage
Inferential tests	Statistical tests that show how a probable or typical a set of data AS A WHOLE is compared to the wider population		
Mann-Whitney U	Compared to the critical value: if lower, the results are significant	Independent groups experiments + ordinal level data	Cannot be used with nominal data; unreliable with small ('5) samples
Wilcoxon	Compared to the critical value: if lower, results are significant	Repeated measures experiments + ordinal level data	Cannot be used with nominal data; unreliable with small ('5) samples
Spearman's Rho	Compared to the critical value: if higher, the results are significant	Used with correlations + ordinal level data	Cannot be used with experiments; doesn't show cause-and-effect
Chi Squared	Compared to the critical value: if higher, results are significant	Independent groups experiments + nominal level data	Cannot be used with ordinal data
Statistical significance	Whether the observed value shows a meaningful difference (experiments) or correlation or whether they are down to chance		
Interval/ratio level	Data where each participant has their own score	Mean can be calculated; can be converted to ordinal level data	Not all behaviours or traits can be expressed as scores; may be REDUCTIONIST
Ordinal level	Data where participants are arranged in rank order, highest to lowest	Median can be calculated; used for Mann-Whitney, Wilcoxon & Spearman	Not all behaviours or traits can be ranked from best to worst; tends to be REDUCTIONIST
Nominal level	Data where behaviours are put into categories (usually as tallies)	Mode can be calculated; used for Chi-Squared	Doesn't show individual scores or performances
Critical value	Score from a statistical table against which the observed value (result of a the test) is compared	Indicates the point where chance variations become signs of a pattern or difference	Critical value varies depending on the LEVEL OF SIGNIFICANCE (probability is usually $p \leq 0.05$)

ISSUES OF STATISTICAL SIGNIFICANCE are covered in **Unit 1**. The typical level is **$p \leq 0.05$** which means ***the probability of a chance outcome is 1 in 20 (5%) or less***. Changing the level of significance alters the critical value. The smaller the value of ***p***, the more probable it is that there is a statistical pattern at work.

GROUNDED THEORY (GLASER & STRAUSS, 1967)

Grounded Theory (GT) is a technique for drawing themes out of qualitative data in a systematic way. It tries to reduce the SUBJECTIVITY (opinion rather than fact) in qualitative data and make the conclusions more OBJECTIVE (factual) while still keeping the depth and detail of qualitative data.

GT was developed by **Glaser & Strauss** while they were researching the experiences of terminally ill patients. Interviewing dying patients is SOCIALLY SENSITIVE so the researchers created this technique to let the patients 'speak for themselves' and avoid imposing their own biases on the data.

GT works by identifying key points in the interview and identifying these with codes. Later, the codes are grouped into similar concepts and categories (referred to as **themes** elsewhere in this course). The researchers create memos (e.g. on file cards) to explore how these categories relate to each other and identify the CORE CATEGORY, which is the basis for a new theory.

This theory is **emergent**: it 'emerges' out of the data rather than being something you start off with. GT can be evaluated in terms of **fitness** (do they 'fit' the data well?), **relevance** (do they tie in with what the respondent feels and wants?), **workability** (can you put them to use?) and **modifiability** (can later research find improve on them?).

- **Freeman *et al.* (2005)** used GT to study how parents try to regulate children's snacking and combat obesity: the core category emerged as 'doing best'
- **Ray (2017)** used GT to study how Indian street children cope with grief when a loved one dies: the core category emerged as 'collective grieving'
- **Lemmer (2017)** used GT to study how fathers are involved in the children's education: the core category emerged as 'improvised leading'

> *You don't need to know much about these studies but it would be good to be able to cite at least one in a discussion of GT*

EVALUATING GROUNDED THEORY IN CHILD PSYCHOLOGY AO3

Glaser and Strauss later disagreed over the role of TRANSCRIPTS in GT. Transcripts are when you write/type up the interview afterwards (creating something that reads like a script of a play). **Barney Glaser** argues that it is time-consuming to create a transcript and you lose the *rapport* (emotional connection) when working from a transcript. **Anselm Strauss** argues that it's easier to come up with codes and write memos when working from a transcript and trying to do these things during the actual interview gets in the way of *rapport* anyway.

This disagreement shows that GT is not a STANDARDISED PROCEDURE (compared to content analysis, for example). This lowers its reliability, because it is hard to replicate, and questions the SCIENTIFIC STATUS of its conclusions.

However, GT is growing in popularity among researchers. **Kathy Charmaz (2006)** has done a lot to bring different approaches to GT together into a usable system. Carmaz adds ORIGINALITY to the ways of evaluating emerging theories:

Are your categories fresh? Do they offer new insights? **– Kathy Charmaz**

GT is useful for interviewing children because it allows the researcher to carry out a natural-sounding **unstructured interview** with a child. It can create **concepts and categories** even if the child has a limited vocabulary or expresses themselves through gestures, facial expressions or drawing. In terms of the **UNCRC**, GT is very useful for increasing children's **participation** in psychological research.

The idea of an **emergent theory** goes against the way scientific research is usually doe (starting with a hypothesis which is tested). GT instead starts with a blank piece of paper and gathers data without trying to fit it into a theory until later. GT aims:

to discover the theory implicit in the data **– Barney Glaser**

This makes GT less useful for testing an established theory (the way **Ainsworth** tested **Bowlby**'s theory of attachment in Uganda and America). However, it can be useful for generating brand new theories because it sets aside biases and preconceptions.

For example, **Bowlby** and **Freud** both went into their research with a theory in mind. Bowlby was expecting to find maternal deprivation in the 'juvenile thieves' and Freud expected to find unconscious conflicts in his patients. Both have been accused of 'cherry picking' their data to get it to back up their theories. If they had used GT instead (if it had existed back then), they might have come up with completely different theories instead!

However, GT might be just a new name for something researchers have always done. **Kanner** and **Asperger** were both able to interview apparently 'retarded' boys and realise that a brand new syndrome of autism was going on, quite separate from low IQ. These men didn't call their approach 'grounded theory' but it seemed to lead to the same results.

REVISING DATA ANALYSIS & GROUNDED THEORY

DEFINITIONS
INTERVAL/RATIO LEVEL DATA
MEAN
MEDIAN
MODE
NOMINAL LEVEL DATA
ORDINAL LEVEL DATA
P≤0.05
RANGE
TRANSCRIPT

WHEN WOULD YOU USE:
CHI-SQUARED
MANN-WHITNEY U TEST
SPEARMAN'S RHO
STANDARD DEVIATION
WILCOXON TEST

RESEARCH
Carry out your own Grounded Theory analysis of a short passage:

- Madie Cardon's diary from when she was 7 describes her crush and heartbreak: it's on several news sites

(type madie+cardon+diary into a search engine)

COMPREHENSION QUESTIONS
1. What are the measures of central tendency?
2. What are the problems with using the mean?
3. What are the measures of dispersion?
4. What is meant by statistical significance?
5. Where do you find a critical value?
6. Which is the stricter test, P≤0.05, P≤0.01 or P≤0.001 ?
7. How do you produce ordinal level data?
8. What sort of data is produced by tally marks in boxes?
9. Who developed Grounded Theory?
10. What is the point of memos in GT?
11. What disagreements are there in using GT?
12. Outline a study that uses GT in Child Psychology.

EXAM-STYLE QUESTIONS

Zaida surveys parents about the positive experiences they have had sending their children to daycare. She scores the number of experiences reported by the first 10 respondents.

(a) Calculate the mode in these scores. [1 mark AO2]

(b) Calculate the standard deviation for these scores. [4 marks, AO2]

(c) Use standard deviation to identify the outliers in these scores. [2 marks AO2]

Participant	Number of Positive Experiences
1	7
2	2
3	6
4	7
5	10
6	2
7	0
8	7
9	5
10	5

CHILD PSYCHOLOGY: STUDIES

What's this topic about?

For your Exam you will need to know about a **classic study** in Child Psychology:

☐ **Van Ijzendoorn & Kroonenberg (1988)**: *Cross-cultural attachment*

Because every candidate studies the same classic study, exam questions could be quite specific (e.g. asking you about the types of attachment in two different countries).

You will also need to know a **contemporary study** and there are 3 to choose from:

☐ **Cassibba *et al.* (2013)**: *Attachment the Italian way*

☐ **Gagnon-Oosterwaal *et al.* (2012)**: *Behaviour problems in 7 year-old international adoptees*

☐ **Li *et al.* (2013)**: *Timing of high-quality daycare*

Because the Examiner doesn't know which contemporary study each candidate has learned, exam questions on the contemporary studies have to be much broader (e.g. just asking for the findings, the procedure or the aims).

---

*However, the **classic** or **contemporary study** could feature in a 16-mark essay question, with up to 10 marks for evaluation (AO3). Therefore, in the next few pages I'll devote more space to evaluating these studies than to describing their procedures or findings in depth.*

WHICH CONTEMPORARY STUDY TO CHOOSE?

☐ **Cassibba *et al.* (2013)** is quite straightforward and follows on from the classic study by **Van Ijzendoorn & Kroonenberg (1988)** in an obvious way. It's another meta-analysis using the **SSP** and it also revisits the **Adult Attachment Interview (AAI)** used by **Koren-Karie (2001)**. It provides you with another **cross-cultural study** to write about, so long as you don't muddle it up with VI+K.

☐ **Gagnon-Oosterwaal *et al.* (2012)** looks at the topic of international adoption and this links into wider debates about **deprivation** during the early critical period and whether **deprivation is reversible**. It introduces some new self-report **questionnaires** and links to topics in Clinical Psychology (**depression** and diagnosis using the **DSM-IV**) and Unit 1 (**phobias**). It's the 'middle study' in terms of difficulty.

☐ **Li *et al.* (2013)** is a **daycare** study using data from the **SECCYD longitudinal study**. This makes it a good addition to the 'Daycare Debate' and it provides examples of **psychometric tests** that can be used on children. However, it's perhaps the most complex study in terms of its procedure and data.

CLASSIC STUDY: VAN IJZENDOORN & KROONENBERG (1988)

This study is a **cross-cultural study** (pp 52, 71) and also a **meta-analysis** (p72) of previous cross-cultural studies using the **Strange Situation Procedure (SSP, p32)**.

> *It's also a pair of longwinded names to spell so I tend to abbreviate it to VI+K.*

AIM

VI+K wanted to test Ainsworth's idea that secure attachment is culturally universal. Ainsworth had found evidence in Uganda and the USA, but during the 1970s and '80s other researchers replicated the SSP in other countries. This meta-analysis brings the separate studies together and draws overall conclusions.

PROCEDURE

This is a meta-analysis so no original (new) research was carried out. Instead, VI+K gathered data from 32 studies in 8 countries, involving nearly 2000 children put through the SSP. VI+K only included studies that used the SSP and Ainsworth's **Type A/B/C classification** (p30) and had a sample size of 35+ consisting of children under 2 years old.

RESULTS

Country	Number of studies	Attachment type (%)		
		Type A (avoidant)	Type B (secure)	Type C (resistant)
USA	18	21	65	14
UK	1	22	75	3
Netherlands	4	26	67	7
Germany	3	35	57	8
Japan	2	5	68	27
China	1	25	50	25
Israel	2	7	64	29
Sweden	1	22	74	4

> *You don't need to memorise the entire table, but revise a couple of stand-out figures from it, like Japan having only 5% Type A but 27% Type C, whereas UK and the Netherlands are the other way around.*

In every country, Type B attachment is the **norm**. However, countries differ in which type of insecure attachment is the second-most-common: in Europe it is Type A, but in Israel and Asia it is Type C; America is 'in the middle' with Type A slightly more common.

- Germany has the highest proportion of Type A attachments (35%, but Type B is still the most common).
- Israel has the highest proportion of Type C attachments (29% but again, Type B is the most common there too).

There were big variations within each country's sample (1.5 times bigger than the differences between one country and another). One study from Germany actually had secure (Type B) attachment as the second-most-common. The data from one Japanese study (in Tokyo) was much closer to the American results than the other Japanese study. Similarly, one Israeli study was from a *kibbutz* but the other Israeli study from a city was more similar to American/European patterns.

CONCLUSIONS

This supports the idea that it is UNIVERSAL for humans to form attachments and that secure attachment is the norm in every culture.

However it suggests there are CULTURAL DIFFERENCES in child-rearing that produce different types of insecure attachment in children. Children are kept sheltered in Asia (and in Israeli *kibbutzim*) and don't meet strangers often; European children are encouraged to be independent, especially in Germany, and are exposed to strangers more.

GENERALISABILITY

SSP studies don't tend to have large samples (since it's difficult to test large numbers of distressed babies!) but every study here included at least 35 and there were 1190 in total, which should stop **anomalies** (exceptionally anxious or placid children) from skewing the results.

Only a single study from a country the size of China cannot possibly be very representative. There are no studies at all from India, South America, Australia or Africa, so this is not a very diverse cross-cultural meta-analysis. Nevertheless, it establishes basic similarities and differences between the USA, Europe and East Asia.

RELIABILITY

The SSP is such a replicable procedure that all the studies VI+K review ***should*** be consistent. However, the SSP is also an **observation** and this means it depends on how the observers interpret behaviour. There might be big differences in how researchers in Japan, Israel and Germany interpret the behaviour of babies and what counts as secure, avoidant and resistant. It's possible that there was no real difference in the babies' behaviour, just a difference in how the researchers were categorising it (e.g. babies who were being categorised as Type B in America were being categorised as Type A in Germany and Type C in Japan).

APPLICATION

Knowing how cultural attitudes to parenting affect attachment might be helpful for daycarers and health professionals to look after children from immigrant families. For example, in a daycentre, carers would expect an Asian child to be more distressed than a German child and give it the right sort of attention (such as a single carer who spends a lot of time in close contact with the child to build its confidence).

However, given the big variations **within** each country in the study, these expectations could just be stereotypes and might lead to children being treated inappropriately (such as a German child's distress being missed because of the stereotype that they are very independent).

VALIDITY

The SSP has been accused of being ETHNOCENTRIC since it is biased in favour of American culture. The idea is that the SSP focuses on distinctively American features of mother-child bonding (such as exploring the world from a 'safe base') and it ignores other features of mother-child bonding that exist in other cultures (like attachment styles other than A/B/C). Therefore, when you test children from other cultures with the SSP, they call come out 'looking American'.

If this is true, then VI+K have not shown real cultural universals. The apparent norm of secure attachment worldwide is produced by the SSP itself, not really present in culture.

ETHICS

The SSP involves causing infants distress by separating them from their mothers and putting them in the presence of a stranger. The **UNCRC** (p78) was only signed the year **after** VI+K's study, but all the countries in the study except America are now signatories to it. The SSP would seem to violate the child's right to **protection** and **provision**.

FURTHER REFLECTIONS

VI+K would be the first to admit that their meta-analysis needs more studies from more countries:

> *Data from less Western-oriented cultures such as Africa, South America and Eastern European socialist countries will be needed to establish a more truly global and better- informed cross-cultural perspective* **– Van Ijzendoorn & Kroonenberg**

They also point out that the Western world mass produces books, TV shows and films promoting its own view of parenting and childhood. Since other cultures consume these media, it might explain why the Western patterns seem to be a worldwide norm and cultural differences are small (link this to **Social Learning Theory** from Unit 1).

89

CONTEMPORARY STUDY 1: CASSIBBA *ET AL.* (2013)

Attachment the Italian Way is the title of this study led by **Rosalinda Cassibba** but including **Marinus Van Ijzendoorn**. It is a **meta-analysis** (p72) of attachment studies from Italy. Italy is strongly (80%) Catholic and religion might help people resolve their attachment issues; it also has more GENDER DIFFERENTIATION (different expectations of males and females) than the USA.

AIM

Identify whether secure attachment is the cultural norm in Italy; identify cultural differences in attachment in Italy compared to the USA norms.

PROCEDURE

Cassibba searched the Internet for 'SSP', 'Italian' and 'attachment'. She included student dissertations and conference papers to avoid the FILE DRAWER PROBLEM, but only used research that had Italian samples and used Ainsworth's **Type A/B/C classification** (p30).

Cassibba also used studies the investigated Italian adults using the **Adult Attachment Interview (AAI**, *c.f.* p40**)**. Adult attachment is categorised in 3 new types:

- **Type D (dismissive-avoidant):** Linked to having Type A children; includes preferring to be independent and not having close relationships with others
- **Type E (anxious-preoccupied):** Linked to having Type C children; includes anxiety about not being appreciated and needing lots of approval
- **Type F (secure autonomous):** Secure attachment to your own children and healthy relationships with others

They selected 17 studies using the SSP and 50 studies using the AAI.

RESULTS

Cassibba looked at attachment distributions for children and for adults and compared them with the USA norms (21 samples based on studies from 1992):

	Child attachment (%)			Mothers attachment (%)		
	A	**B**	**C**	**D**	**E**	**F**
Italian	33	53	14	22	19	59
USA	21	67	12	23	19	58

As usual, don't memorise the entire table but revise the standout figures, like 33% of Italian children being Type A compared to 21% of American children.

Cassibba also looked at hospitalised children separately and found much higher insecure attachment (only 32% were securely attached Type B).

Cassibba also looked at Italian fathers (higher Type Ds and fewer Type Fs, so more dismissive and less secure) and adolescents (slightly more type Ds but fewer Type Es, so more dismissive but less anxious).

CONCLUSIONS

There is strong evidence for UNIVERSALITY in attachment styles because the Italian patterns are very similar to the American patterns (especially the mothers tested on the AAI). Secure attachment is the most common type for children and adults.

Attachment seems to be linked to separation and mental health, with children in clinical care being less securely attached. This supports **Bowlby**'s theory of maternal deprivation (p25). However, there is evidence for cultural differences too. As a European country, Italians fit the pattern of valuing independence so insecure Type A attachment is higher than in the USA. Cassibba suggests that Italian mothers see development as something that happens naturally, so they are less 'hands on' than American mothers.

There are gender differences in attachment, with fathers being more Type D (dismissive); however, secure Type F is still the most common style for males. Adolescents show signs of this tendency towards Type D, but are also less anxious than Americans. Cassibba suggests religion plays a role in helping adolescents cope.

> *Cassibba et al. also studied the amount of Type D (disorganised) attachment in children and Type U (unresolved, mentally ill) attachment in adults and found Italians to be healthier than Americans but I've not included all the details here.*

GENERALISABILITY

With 67 studies and nearly 3000 participants, anomalies will not skew the results greatly. However, as usual, samples for SSP studies tend to be small, so 78% of the sample was adults taking the AAI rather than children.

This study presents Italians as a HOMOGENOUS (unified) culture but there is a difference between the North (wealthy, urban, stereotypically 'colder' people) and the South (poorer, urban, stereotypically 'warmer' people).

RELIABILITY

The US norm was worked out in 1992 and is very similar to the figures used by **Van Ijzendoorn & Kroonenberg (1988**, p87**)** and **Ainsworth**'s original findings (**1978**). This suggests the American patterns are consistent and reliable and provide a baseline for comparison.

There are problems with relying on a **semi-structured interview** like the AAI which allows interviewers to influence how interviewees answer (and since Cassibba used unpublished student dissertations, some of this research might not have been done professionally).

APPLICATION

The results of this study could help Italian social services provide better childcare. Knowing that children in care are insecurely attached could trigger interventions to provide more one-on-one carer (which would involve more Government spending). The role of religion in helping Italians cope with adolescence could justify involving the Catholic Church more in youth projects and helping youth offenders (e.g. drugs rehab).

VALIDITY

There are unexplained variables in the data. For example, why is Type D attachment so common in Italian fathers? This might be a result of Mediterranean 'macho' culture – and a survey from 2011 by the 'Women & Quality of Life' think tank found that Italian women were *"the unhappiest in Europe"* because of the lack of support from Italian men (70% have never used an oven, 95% have never emptied a washing machine, apparently).

However, it might be that Italian men are just uncomfortable answering the questions in the AAI. A question like *"think of five adjectives that reflect your relationship with your mother"* might be difficult to answer in a Catholic culture that rates motherhood highly. If men give stereotyped and under-developed answers, they could be wrongly coded as Type D because they don't demonstrate intimacy in the interview.

ETHICS

This is a meta-analysis so no original research was carried out. However, there are ethical concerns with the SSP which involves putting babies in distressing situations. Italy is a signatory to the **UNCRC (1989)**.

FURTHER REFLECTIONS

This study supports the conclusions of **Van Ijzendoorn & Kroonenberg (1988)**, which is that European countries value independence in children; mothers are more willing to let children out of their supervision and allow them to encounter strangers. This leads to more Type A attachments. 33% Type A is right up there with Germany's 35% from VI+K.

Cassibba paints a picture of 'hands-off' Italian mothers who let their children roam, but a supportive Catholic religion that 'picks up the pieces' and gives older children and adolescents a sense of belonging.

However, Cassibba does not consider the role of fathers in these patterns. The high proportion of Type A children might be a result of their dismissive (aloof, unapproachable) fathers, rather than anything the mothers do. It would be interesting to break the results down by gender to see if boys respond more to the father's attachment style and girls to the mother's style (as predicted by **Bandura's Social Learning Theory** from Unit 1).

CONTEMPORARY STUDY 2: GAGNON-OOSTERWAAL *ET AL.* (2012)

Behaviour problems in 7 year-old international adoptees is the title of this study led by **Noémi Gagnon-Oosterwaal**. PRE-ADOPTION ADVERSITY means that international adoptees have come from a different country and have often spent a long time in institutional care (orphanages) before being adopted.

AIM

Determine if international adoptees (IAs) have more behavioural problems than non-adopted children and what sort of problems these are.

PROCEDURE

The sample was 95 children (69 girls, 26 boys) adopted in Quebec, Canada when they were under 18 months old. They were originally from China (50%), elsewhere in East Asia (30%), Russia (18%), Haiti and Bolivia (1% each). Canadian authorities gathered medical data on the children when they arrived. The researchers gathered more data when the children were 7 years old:

- **Child Behavioural Checklist (CBCL):** This questionnaire was completed by the mothers; there are 118 closed questions (choose from *not true*, *sometimes true* and *very true*); the questions identify INTERNALISING PROBLEMS (e.g. depression, anxiety, pain) or EXTERNALISING PROBLEMS (e.g. aggression, rule-breaking)
- **Dominic Interactive (DI):** A computer test that shows 94 pictures and the child clicks *Yes* or *No* based on whether they think, feel or act like the picture; the results link to the DSM-IV (*c.f.* Unit 2A Clinical Psychology) and diagnose depressive disorders, separation anxiety, phobias and other problems.

The results were compared to a Control Group of 41 non-adopted Canadian children.

RESULTS

	Self-reported symptoms (%)	
	Internalising	**Externalising**
IAs	43	31
Controls	29	22

The main difference in internalising symptoms is **phobias** (33% of IAs compared to 7% of controls) but **separation anxiety** and **depression** are also slightly more common.

The main difference in externalising symptoms is **oppositional defiance disorder** (tantrums, 22% compared to 12%) but the IAs actually report less **ADHD** (hyperactivity, 11% compared to 17%).

The researchers found no significant gender differences but they did find a significant **correlation** between the mother's assessments of the child's externalising problems and the child's self report (significant to **p≤0.001**).

Health records showed a significant **correlation** between the child's **height/weight ratio** when they entered Canada and symptoms of **depression** (-0.21) and **phobias** (-0.23), both at p≤0.05 significance.

CONCLUSIONS

The majority of IAs are well-adjusted and do not report problems. Gagnon-Oosterwaal proposes that those reporting phobias and anxiety are still suffering from the poor care they received before they were adopted. However, **Levy-Shiff et al. (1997)** suggests that the adoptive parents of IAs tend to be over-protective and this could promote phobias and anxiety too.

The correlation between size and internalising problems suggests that these IAs were under-nourished at the time of their arrival, which indicates poor care.

The low levels of ADHD and other behavioural problems might be because many of the IAs were girls from China and Chinese girls tend to show fewer behavioural problems.

Parents' assessments of their children's externalising problems are trustworthy – which is good because most studies into IAs rely on parental reports rather than the children.

GENERALISABILITY

Selman (2013) shows that the main countries sending IAs abroad for the last decade have been China followed by Ethiopia, India, South Korea, Ukraine and Vietnam. Gagnon-Oosterwaal's sample matches this for Chinese and East Asian (Korean and Vietnamese) IAs but does not include any from Africa or India. Therefore the sample may not be representative of IAs worldwide.

RELIABILITY

The CBCL and DI questionnaires are standardised procedures used in many other studies. However, Gagnon-Oosterwaal found that the accuracy of parent's assessments went down when they were stressed (e.g. by behavioural problems in their children) and it's possible that the children's self-reports using DI were influenced by their adoptive parents' view of them. If stressed parents told the IAs that they were badly behaved and the children believed this, then the results become unreliable.

APPLICATION

The study is very useful for families deciding whether to adopt internationally. Previous studies (e.g. **Miller, 2000**) suggested that IAs came with all sorts of behavioural and emotional problems that adoptive parents struggle to help with. Gagnon-Oosterwaal's conclusions are more upbeat, with only phobias standing out as a significant problem for IAs compared to non-adopted peers. The correlation involving height/weight ratio suggests a way of identifying children who will have the worst problems so that they can be placed with adoptive parents who can offer the best care.

VALIDITY

The main problem with this study is deciding whether the IAs problems are created by PRE-ADOPTION ADVERSITY (i.e. the terrible conditions in the orphanages they came from) or from the over-protective and over-controlling behaviour of the adoptive parents. It's understandable that families adopting IAs would be very conscious of the child having suffered greatly and respond by 'wrapping them in cotton wool' and this could be the real cause of anxiety disorders and phobias.

ETHICS

The IAs took part in this study with the presumptive consent of their adoptive parents, who also agreed for the health records to be shared. International adoption is a SOCIALLY SENSITIVE issue (p110), so research that suggests it is stressful for the parents or damaging for the child could have negative repercussions for a lot of children.

FURTHER REFLECTIONS

International adoption is promoted by some celebrities (like Madonna and Angelina Jolie). Potential adopters want to know if IAs will be permanently damaged by their deprived backgrounds – and need to be advised if their own over-protective parenting adds to the problem.

This study has implications for the debate about whether deprivation is reversible: "*Yes, but not completely*" because more than half of the IAs reported no problems and those who did report problems were not significantly more troubled than their non-adopted peers. However, phobias stand out and the correlation with early malnutrition suggests this is connected to deprivation.

International adoption seems to be declining. There were 1379 international adoptions in Canada in 2012, but this dropped to 793 in 2016 (source: CBS News). Reasons include more focus on domestic adoption and new fertility treatments. China has relaxed its 'One Child Policy' and puts less pressure on families to give up their children and Russia under Vladimir Putin has restricted adoption by countries that allow same-sex marriage.

CONTEMPORARY STUDY 3: LI *ET AL.* (2013)

Timing of high-quality daycare is the title of this study led by **Weilin Li**. High-quality daycare involves small group sizes, high staff-to-child ratios, trained staff and stimulating activities. She used data from the recently ended **SECCYD longitudinal study** (p39).

AIM

Determine whether early high-quality daycare provides a 'boost' for children which lasts until school age or whether later high-quality daycare can make up for low-quality daycare earlier in infancy.

PROCEDURE

The study used 1364 families with babies born in 1991 taking part in the SECCYD longitudinal study. The sample drew from 10 US locations and different races and social classes, including teenage mothers, disabled children and non-English speakers.

Children were assessed for health, child temperament and family background. Daycare was assessed as high/low quality using the **Observation Record of Caregiving Environment (ORCE)** test (a 45 minute **naturalistic observation** every year).

- **Infant/toddler period** assessed at 24 months (2 years) using the **Bayley Mental Development Index** to measure IQ
- **Pre-school period** assessed at 54 months (4½ years) using **Woodcock-Johnson Tests** for memory, language, reading and Maths.

The children were in 4 conditions (a **natural experiment**):

1. **High→Low:** High-quality daycare as infants, low-quality as pre-schoolers
2. **Low→High:** Low-quality daycare as infants, high-quality as pre-schoolers
3. **High→High:** High-quality daycare as infants all the way through to pre-schoolers
4. **Low→Low:** Low-quality daycare as infants all the way through to pre-schoolers

RESULTS

The infants who started in high-quality daycare score 28% higher on average than infants in low-quality daycare on the IQ tests (significant to $p \leq 0.001$). High→Low lost this superiority by the time of pre-school, except for memory (+20%, just $p \leq 0.01$).

High→High vs...	Pre-school Woodcock-Johnson Test for:		
	Language	**Reading**	**Maths**
Low→Low	+35% ($p \leq 0.001$)	+17% ($p \leq 0.01$)	+28% ($p \leq 0.001$)
High→Low	+21% ($p \leq 0.05$)		
Low→High		+20% ($p \leq 0.01$)	

> *Make sure you understand that p≤0.001 means that the results are MORE significant than p≤0.01 and that p≤0.05 is LESS significant than the others. A blank space means the High→High students had no significant advantage in this category.*

CONCLUSIONS

Putting children into daycare as infant/toddlers gives an early boost to IQ but this fades if children move into low-quality daycare (except for memory scores, which remain better).

Keeping children in high-quality daycare from infancy through to pre-school gives them an academic advantage over children who stay in low-quality daycare in everything except memory.

However, it's not as clear-cut when compared to other children who started in high-quality daycare (who remain equal on reading and Maths) or who moved into high-quality daycare later (who catch up on language and Maths).

Any sort of exposure to high-quality daycare (whether in infancy or pre-school) seems to be beneficial for children but p≤0.01 means that the reading benefit from Low→High is less likely to be down to chance than the language benefit from High→Low.

GENERALISABILITY

As a longitudinal study drawing from several US states, from cities and the countryside and a diverse range of family types, the results should be representative of American society. However, although diverse, this is not a **stratified sample** since the proportions of different races, class backgrounds etc. do not exactly match the proportions in American society as a whole.

The SECCYD **longitudinal study** ran from 1991 to 2009, therefore this data was 4 years old when Li *et al.* used it.

RELIABILITY

The SECCYD ran for 18 years using standardised procedures and well-tested instruments (like the Bayley Index and Woodcock-Johnson Tests). The ORCE is a reliable observational tool for measuring the quality of daycare (score 3.0 or higher means an environment with sensitive caring and cognitive stimulation).

APPLICATION

This is a very useful study for helping parents make decisions about daycare. It shows that high-quality daycare is good value for money as children benefit clearly in academic tests. If parents are struggling to avoid high-quality daycare, it suggests that low-quality early daycare followed by high-quality daycare after age 2 has a slightly more certain benefit.

Li *et al.* argue that governments should use this research to provide more funding for high-quality daycare, but that if funding bodies has to choose between daycare in the infant/toddler period and daycare in the pre-school period, they should fund high-quality pre-school daycare.

VALIDITY

Using the information about the children and their home background in the first year of life, Li *et al.* were able to control for confounding variables like the child's temperament, the mother having depression or things like race and gender. Nevertheless, there are so many variables and no two children's circumstances are ever identical so the comparisons in this study may not be entirely valid.

Similarly, high and low quality daycare was determined by whether the daycare scored 3.0+ on ORCE. This is **reductionist** as daycare varies, no two places are identical and the relationship between carers and children changes all the time.

ETHICS

The parents and daycarers gave presumptive consent for the children to be studied. Nevertheless, being tested at such a young age can be stressful and children who do poorly on these tests may suffer loss of confidence.

FURTHER THOUGHTS

This study focuses on cognitive development and academic skills, but critics of daycare like **Jay Belsky** are more concerned about behavioural problems and aggression, which Li *et al.* don't investigate.

This is an American study, but can it be generalised to the UK? Studies like **Van Ijzendoorn & Kroonenberg (1988**, p87**)** show British children to be slightly more securely attached than Americans, with fewer Type C attachments, but with broadly the same pattern of attachment.

The *Doing Better for Families* report (**OECD, 2011**) found UK daycare to be the most expensive in Europe (27% of family income, compared to 23% in the USA and 10-11% in France and Germany), so British families will struggle to afford high-quality daycare right the way from infancy to pre-school (i.e. High→High).

However, the UK Government now offers free daycare for 3-4 year-olds (i.e. the pre-school period) so British families are more likely receive Low→High if they cannot afford High→High. Li *et al.* would say that the UK Government has made the right choice to fund this pre-school phase of childcare rather than the infancy phase.

REVISING CLASSIC & CONTEMPORARY STUDIES

DEFINITIONS: VI+K
COLLECTIVIST
INDIVIDUALISTIC
NORM
SSP
TYPE A/B/C CLASSIFICATION

DEFINITIONS: CASSIBA ET AL.
AAI
TYPE D/E/F CLASSSIFICATION
TYPE U CLASSIFICATION

DEFINITIONS : GAGNON-OOSTERWAAL ET AL.
CBCL
DI
IA
PRE-ADOPTION ADVERSITY

DEFINITIONS : LI ET AL.
BAYLEY MENTAL DEVELOPMENT INDEX
INFANT/TODDLER PERIOD
ORCE
PRE-SCHOOL PERIOD
WOODCOCK-JOHNSON TESTS

RESEARCH
Find out about China's One Child Policy and its after-effects

TICK YOUR CONTEMPORARY STUDY
☐ CASSIBA ET AL. (2013) Attachment the Italian way
☐ GAGNON-OOSTERWAAL ET AL. (2012) International adoptees
☐ LI ET AL (2013) High quality daycare

COMPREHENSION QUESTIONS
VI+K
1. What was unusual about the results from Germany?
2. What was unusual about the results from Japan?
3. How do VI+K explain the similarity of the results across cultures?
4. How do they explain the differences?
CASSIBA ET AL.
5. What was the sample?
6. How does Italian attachment differ from American attachment styles?
GAGNON-OOSTERWAAL ET AL.
7. How did the IAs differ from their non-adopted peers?
8. What two explanations are there for this?
LI ET AL.
9. How did children in high-quality daycare perform better on tests?
10. Explain whether the effects of early high-quality daycare last into pre-school.

EXAM-STYLE QUESTIONS

As part of Child Psychology, you learned about the classic study by Van Ijzendoorn & Kroonenberg (1988).

(a) Describe the findings (results and/or conclusions) of this study relating to non-Western cultures. [4 marks AO1]

(b) Explain one strength and one weakness of the study's Israeli and/or Japanese samples. [4 marks AO3]

(c) Evaluate the contemporary study you learned about for Child Psychology. [8 marks AO1+AO3 or 16 marks AO1+AO3]

CHILD PSYCHOLOGY: KEY QUESTIONS

What's this topic about?

For the Exam, you need to know about

> *one issue of relevance to today's society, explaining the issue and applying concepts, theories and/or research (as appropriate) drawn from child psychology* — **Edexcel Specification, p36**

Two examples are offered:

☐ What issues should parents take into account when deciding about day care for their child?

☐ Is international adoption good or bad for a child?

Notice that this is a KEY QUESTION and these really are QUESTIONS. If the Exam asks you to write your Key Question, you won't get marks unless you write it as a question, not just "daycare" or "international adoptions"

For your Key Question, you must be able to

- show some **real-world knowledge** of these topics (not studies or theories but actual news events, Government policies or statistical trends in society)

- show how **psychological studies or theories** explain these real-world facts

This is important. If you just treat the Key Question as an essay on "the psychology of daycare" or "the psychology of adoption" you will lose a lot of marks.

The next two pages offer 4 'facts' for each of the suggested Key Questions. Students could research these facts a bit further. There are also pointers to the psychological theories and studies in this book that link to these 'facts'.

KEY QUESTION 1: What issues should parents take into account when deciding about day care for their child?

FACT 1: Daycare is expensive

The UK has the highest costs of childcare for any European country apart from Switzerland according to the *Doing Better for Families* report (OECD, 2011). 67% of British mothers return to work compared to 84% in Denmark and 74% in France. This suggests the cost of daycare is keeping mothers at home.

- **Psychology link:** What research suggests children might benefit if mothers do not return to work early? Which studies offer advice on the funding of childcare?

FACT 2: The UK Government funds daycare

Since 2010, the UK Government funds places in daycare for all 3-4 year-olds. Working families can get 15-30 hours of daycare free. The Government does this to hep mothers return to work and to boost children's attainment when they start school.

- **Psychology link:** What research supports funding daycare for 3-4 year-olds? What studies suggest they will benefit or suffer from being put in daycare?

FACT 3: Daycare is dropping in quality

The Good Care Guide is a website that lets parents rate the quality of childcare. Between 2012-16, ratings for daycare went down, for reasons like high turnover of staff, children not learning enough and small rooms with lack of stimulation. This might be due to the low pay for carers leading to a lack of educated staff.

- **Psychology link:** What are the effects of low-quality daycare on children? What studies prove this?

FACT 4: There are alternatives to daycare

One is bringing your baby with you to work. In 2017, Australian senator Larissa Waters became the first person to breastfeed a baby in parliament. There's no culture of bringing babies into work in the UK but the Parenting in the Workplace Institute signs up companies to a "babies at work" policy and more than 200 participate.

- **Psychology link:** What research suggests some mothers should keep their babies close? What sort of mothers and what sort of babies would benefit from this?

KEY QUESTION 2: Is international adoption good or bad for a child?

FACT 1: Parents often can't cope with international adoptees (IAs)

In 2010, a woman from Tennessee, USA put her adopted 7-year-old Russian boy on a plane back to Moscow, giving him a letter saying she was returning him because *"this child is mentally unstable – he is violent and has severe psychopathic issues."* The outcry about this led to Russia banning international adoptions from the USA temporarily.

- **Psychology link:** What research suggests children adopted from abroad might have long-term issues?

FACT 2: Adoptive parents can abuse IAs

In 2008, a 21-month-old toddler died when his adoptive American father left him strapped in the back of his car for 9 hours in July heat because he forgot to drop him off at daycare. Russian leaders questioned whether sending children abroad is in their best interests when a US court acquitted the father of manslaughter after hearing that he had been a loving parent.

- **Psychology link:** What theories suggest parents may not bond with IAs or that IAs may not be responsive to their adoptive parents?

FACT 3: Countries are cutting back on international adoption

China used to be the leader in sending adopted children abroad but since 2015 China has cut back foreign adoptions by 86%; South Korea and Russia are doing the same. Some of this is political (like Russia refusing to send adoptees to countries with same-sex marriage) but some of it is a cultural change (like China ending its 'One Child Policy').

- **Psychology link:** What research suggests children will suffer if they remain in institutions and are not adopted?

FACT 4: Poor children benefit from international adoption

IAs are often coming from countries with poor rates of literacy and child mortality to live in richer countries where they are educated and receive good healthcare. Actress Angelina Jolie has adopted children from Cambodia, Ethiopia and Vietnam; Madonna has adopted two children from Malawi.

- **Psychology link:** What research suggests that middle-class parents offer superior childcare? What about the benefits of high-quality daycare?

CHILD PSYCHOLOGY: PRACTICAL INVESTIGATION

What's this topic about?

To prepare for the Exam, you need to

> *conduct one study using a questionnaire, interview or observation* **– Edexcel Specification, p37**

Two examples are offered:

- ☐ Interview of an adult to look for a relationship between strong attachment experiences and strong adult relationships.

- ☐ Interview of a parent of a child under 3 years old around positive experiences when using day care for their child.

> *Notice that you are advised to interview an ADULT. The Examiner expects you to follow BPS Guidelines and not to carry out research on children under 16.*

For your Key Question, you must be able to

- • Gather quantitative data and carry out an inferential statistical test

- • Describe the hypotheses being tested, sample, procedure & instruments used, results and conclusions

- • Discuss the strengths, weaknesses and possible improvements

> *This is important. The Exam is more likely to ask you to EVALUATE your Practical than it is to ask you to describe what you did or what you found.*

The next two pages offer guidelines for carrying out the suggested Practicals. You only need to do one and you should keep it as simple as possible. Make sure you understand **why** you are doing what you are doing by answering the questions too..

PRACTICAL 1: A relationship between strong attachment experiences and strong adult relationships

HYPOTHESIS

There will be a significant positive correlation between participants' scores for their own attachment and scores for the strength of their adult relationships.

- Is this 1-tailed or 2-tailed? Design a null hypothesis based on this.

SAMPLE

Either gather an opportunity sample of students at your Centre or a volunteer sample of friends who respond through social media. Make sure everyone gives informed consent and is 16+.

- Examine the critical value tables (at the start of each Exam Paper): how many participants do you need to carry out a successful inferential test?

INSTRUMENTS

The Adult Attachment Scale (AAS): **http://www.statisticssolutions.com/adult-attachment-scale-aas/**

Just count the scores of 'secure' (S) questions and ignore the rest to get a value for the strength of attachment

Relationship Strength Quiz: **https://psychcentral.com/quizzes/relationship-quiz/**

This measures the strength of a romantic relationship or friendship. However, you can get a 'quick'n'easy' score by just asking participants to count the number of close friends they have in their life.

INFERENTIAL TEST

Use Spearman's Rho to measure a correlation between the two scores.

- Why is Spearman's Rho the appropriate test to use in this case?

DISCUSSION

Evaluate your sample: How would a different sample size, target population or sampling technique have improved things?

Evaluate the questions asked: Do any pose ethical problems? Are any of them vague or misleading? could an observation have produced a better score for one of the variables?

PRACTICAL 2: Positive experiences when using daycare

HYPOTHESIS

One type of parent will score higher for positive experiences when using daycare than another type of parent.

- What types of parent will you approach: mothers vs fathers? 20-somethings vs 30-somethings? single vs couples? full-time daycare-users vs part-time?

- Is this 1-tailed or 2-tailed? Design a null hypothesis based on this.

SAMPLE

Either gather an opportunity sample of parents through family friends or ask other students with young siblings to survey their own parents. Alternatively, reach out to parents through social media.

- Examine the critical value tables (at the start of each Exam Paper): how many participants do you need to carry out a successful inferential test?

INSTRUMENTS

Sample parental questionnaire: **https://education.gov.scot/Documents/questionnaires-for-ELC-settings.pdf**

There are 27 Likert-style questions in this questionnaire but you should cut the list down to the 10 most appropriate questions.

> *Notice how this questionnaire focuses on POSITIVE experiences. If you design your own self report, you should have the same focus.*

INFERENTIAL TEST

Use Mann-Whitney U Test to measure a difference between the two types of parents.

- Why is Mann-Whitney U Test the appropriate test to use in this case?

DISCUSSION

Evaluate your sample: How would a different sample size, target population or sampling technique have improved things?

Evaluate the questions asked: Do any pose ethical problems? Are any of them vague or misleading? Could an observation or an interview have produced a better score? What would have been the advantages of researching the children rather than the parents?

CHILD PSYCHOLOGY: ISSUES & DEBATES

What's this topic about?

These 11 'Issues & Debates' can feature as part of a question in Unit 2C as well as a question related to Applications in Unit 3 (Issues & Debates).

COMPARING EXPLANATIONS WITH DIFFERENT THEMES

Learning Theory (Behaviourism, p12) is an explanation for all human behaviour in terms of stimulus and response; it can be applied to attachment. It claims that children become attached to the person who rewards them with food (the CUPBOARD LOVE explanation).

Psychodynamic Theory (Freudianism, p10) also explains all human behaviour in terms of instincts and unconscious desires. It claims that children have instinctive desires for pleasure that they receive from their mother's presence.

Bowlby's theory of attachment (p25) brings these themes together, arguing that children form attachments to carers who comfort them rather than those who simply feed them. However, they can learn new attachments besides the one with their mother. Bowlby takes the Freudian idea that our first mother-attachment shapes our INTERNAL WORKING MODEL (p20) that influences all future relationships. However, he rejects Freud's focus on studying feelings and desires in favour of the more SCIENTIFIC behaviourist idea that attachment is a set of observable behaviours.

CULTURE

A culture is a group of people united by common norms, beliefs and practices. For example, British culture unites people are norms like politeness and drinking tea, beliefs in democracy and individualism and practices like football, following soap operas and eating fish & chips. It's sometimes common to talk of 'Western culture' meaning the norms, beliefs and practices uniting Europe, North America and Australia. This is often described as an INDIVIDUALIST CULTURE that emphasises interval people over the group; Asian and African culture is described as COLLECTIVIST, with less focus on individuals than groups.

In Child Psychology, the main effect of culture you have studied is on attachment styles, with individualist cultures tending more towards Type A and collectivist cultures towards Type C.

ETHNOCENTRISM is the belief that your own culture is normal or natural, e.g. that the attachment styles that are the norm in your culture are also UNIVERSAL. This is a form of bias that can be corrected through cross-cultural research.

ETHICS

Ethics are rules that oblige us to ensure the wellbeing of other people (and also animals). Ethical guidelines were developed by the **British Psychological Society (BPS)** in 1974 but in 1989 these were supplemented by the **United Nations Convention on the Rights of the Child (UNCRC**, p78**)**. These ethical codes insist that children be **protected** and **provided for** while at the same time having their right to **participate** in research and their **privacy** respected (the FOUR Ps).

Ainsworth's Strange Situation Procedure (SSP, p32**)** is ethically controversial as it deliberately causes distress for children by removing their mothers then exposing them to strangers. Under BPS Guidelines, this could be justified if the research was of benefit to society and the parents consented on the child's behalf; it's less clear how this could be justified under the stricter UNCRC code.

The case study of Genie by **Curtiss (1977**, p16**)** illustrates this ethical problem in a more extreme way. Genie was a deeply traumatised child who required love and security but researchers treated her instead like a guinea pig for testing and her wellbeing was not ensured.

NATURE-NURTURE

'Nature' is a term for aspects of human identity that we are born with (INNATE) whereas 'nurture' is a term for aspects of identity that we learn from our environment. Human identity seems to be a mixture of nature e.g. our genes) and nurture (e.g. our upbringing) but psychologists debate which is more influential.

Cross-cultural research (pp52, 71) shows that forming secure attachments seems to be natural for humans, but some babies might have temperaments that make this more difficult for them than others. However, the sensitivity and responsiveness of the parent is part of nurture and this can cause a child to develop different sorts of insecure attachment.

Case studies of FERAL CHILDREN (p15) show us what happens to human children who do not experience nurture at a critical age in infancy. Psychologists debate whether the experience of nurture in later childhood can reverse this damage.

PRACTICAL ISSUES IN DESIGNING RESEARCH

The main practical issue in Child Psychology is that children cannot communicate their own thoughts and feelings to researchers. In the case of infants, this is because they haven't developed language yet; in the case of older children, their language may be limited, their understanding of questions may be flawed or they may be too influenced by the desire to please adults (DEMAND CHARACTERISTICS) to respond truthfully.

Many psychologists respond to this challenge by observing children rather than communicating with them directly. **Structured observations** like the SSP can set up situations designed to reveal the child's relationships and reactions in a clear light. **Naturalistic observations** in the home, nursery or hospital can observe how the child reacts to others. **Longitudinal studies** can repeat these observations over time to detect changing relationships and reactions.

However, **questionnaires** have been developed for children. Some of these are **psychometric tests** (often involving pictures rather than words) which indicate a child's IQ or other abilities. **Interviews** with adults can reveal the INTERNAL WORKING MODEL (p20) formed by childhood experiences, even if those experiences have been forgotten.

PSYCHOLOGY DEVELOPS OVER TIME

The key figures in the development of Child Psychology are **John Bowlby** (p25) and **Mary Ainsworth** (p30). Bowlby brought together a Freudian interest in the mother-child bond with insights from ETHOLOGY (the study of animal behaviour) and aspects of Learning Theory. His ideas of attachment have shaped everything that came after, even though some of his specific ideas (like the absolute importance of the bond with the mother in the first 18 months of life) have been questioned and Bowlby himself abandoned them.

Ainsworth took Bowlby's ideas and tested them in Africa and America. She developed the **Strange Situation Procedure (SSP**, p32**)** to show that there were different styles of attachment and that these were influenced by the sensitivity and responsiveness of the parent. The SSP have been replicated in many studies, extending the cross-cultural comparisons of different attachment styles.

The current debate in Child Psychology rages over DAYCARE (p36). **Jay Belsky (1986)** warned that daycare could damage children and this launched three decades of research involving huge longitudinal studies (e.g. **SECCYD** in the USA and **EPPE** in Britain) that have increased our understanding of how children develop based on sensitivity and stimulation.

REDUCTIONISM

Reductionism is reducing an explanation of human behaviour to a simple level to understand it better. This can be done through reducing human traits to number scores (quantitative data) or putting human behaviour into one of a small number of categories or types. Reductionism is an essential component of SCIENTIFIC explanations.

Child Psychology is reductionist when it reduces children to number scores (e.g. IQ) or defines them entirely by their age (as if all 12 month old babies were the same). **Ainsworth's Type A/B/C classification** (p30) can be seen as reductionist as is **Baron-Cohen**'s explanation of autism as the **Extreme Male Brain** (p45).

However, child psychologists are alert to the danger of this and now try to include as many variables as possible in their research. The big **longitudinal** studies like **SECCYD** (p39) gather data on the child's physical, emotional and mental traits, the home background, the parents' relationships, etc. The aim is to make research less reductionist while still ensuring it is scientific.

SCIENTIFIC STATUS

Science is a method for investigating the world in an OBJECTIVE (detached, factual) way. Scientific research tests HYPOTHESES to develop THEORIES which account for things in a systematic, rules-based way. It is a very successful way of discovering truth and solving problems.

Psychology is termed a 'social science' but there are problems with studying humans – and especially children – scientifically. Humans are RESPONSIVE and react to what you do to them; they are MORALLY SIGNIFICANT which restricts what you are allowed to do with them; and they are AUTONOMOUS which means they can choose how to act rather than being governed by simple laws of cause-and-effect.

From the work of Bowlby onwards, Child Psychology has tried to develop more and more scientific ways of studying the nature of childhood while still respecting the responsive, morally significant and autonomous nature of children and adults. For example, the **SSP** allows children to respond to the departure of their mother and the arrival of a stranger in a way that can be studied objectively (albeit with ethical problems).

SOCIAL CONTROL

The hand that rocks the cradle is the hand that rules the world – **William Ross Wallace**

Wallace's famous quote means that, if you have power over people while they are children, you can influence the sort of adults they turn into. If you have power over enough children, you can influence the way the world will be in the future.

Child Psychology tries to use this power for good: to help children develop secure attachments and experience stimulation so that they can grow into healthy and AUTONOMOUS (free-willed) adults.

However, psychological ideas can be used to change people in other ways. In the *kibbutzim* of Israel, children were raised away from their parents so that they would grow up to be attached to each other and to their new country. *Kibbutzim* have largely dropped this approach since the 1980s but other governments (Communist and Fascist) have tried to break the attachment between child and parent in order better to control the child when it grows up. For example, the terrorist group Boko Haram abducts children to become child soldiers in Nigeria and trains them to be suicide bombers.

SOCIAL SENSITIVITY

This is when research has implications that go beyond participating in the study itself, either long-term harm for the participants or harmful influence on society itself.

A famous example of this is Bowlby's research into maternal deprivation. **Bowlby** argued that children needed a monotropic bond with their mother and were damaged if they didn't form a healthy attachment in their early years. After WWII, when men returned from the War to the workforce, there was pressure on women to give up the jobs they had been doing and go back to being mothers and housewives. Bowlby's ideas were used (although not by Bowlby himself) to frighten women with the idea that they were damaging their children by selfishly insisting on keeping their independence.

Bowlby also argued that *"a bad home is better for a child than a good institution"* and his theories made social services reluctant to remove children from their families, even if this meant leaving children where they would be neglected or abused.

Bowlby himself modified his ideas (allowing that the child could bond with more than one carer, including fathers, and that deprivation could be reversed by later loving support) but the harmful influence had already taken place.

USEFULNESS IN SOCIETY

A useful application is the **Sure Start Programme** in the UK which was founded in 1998. Sure Start runs 3000 day centres for children of up to age 4 and also provides classes for parents in parenting techniques. It is based on the **Head Start** project in the USA which has been running since the 1960s. Sure Start is intended to help improve the success of children from poorer backgrounds when they start school by improving cognitive skills, social skills and emotional development.

Sure Start Children's Centres

Sure Start has been criticised for not producing measurable benefits for children when they start school. However, its supporters say that it has been under-funded and not properly targeted at poor families (middle class parents tend to take up the subsidised daycare places instead).

REVISING KEY QUESTIONS, PRACTICALS & ISSUES

DEFINITIONS

CULTURE
ETHICS
INFERENTIAL TEST
HYPOTHESIS
NATURE-NURTURE
NULL HYPOTHESIS
OPERATIONALISE
PRACTICAL DESIGN ISSUES
PSYCHOLOGY OVER TIME
REDUCTIONISM
SCIENTIFIC STATUS
SOCIAL CONTROL
SOCIAL SENSITIVITY
SOCIAL USEFULNESS
TEST OF CORRELATION
TEST OF DIFFERENCE

TICK YOUR KEY QUESTION

☐ WHAT ISSUES SHOULD PARENTS TAKE INTO ACCOUNT WHEN DECIDING ON DAYCARE FOR THEIR CHILD?

☐ IS INTERNATIONAL ADOPTION GOOD OR BAD FOR A CHILD?

TICK YOUR PRACTICAL

☐ INTERVIEW LOOKING FOR RELATIONSHIP BETWEEN ATTACHMENT EXPERIENCES & ADULT RELATIONSHIPS

☐ INTERVIEW LOOKING FOR DIFFERENCES IN POSITIVE EXPERIENCES OF DAYCARE

EXAM-STYLE QUESTIONS

(a) Discuss the key question you have researched in Child Psychology. [8 marks AO1+AO2]

(b) (i) Explain the method (aims and/or procedures) you used in your Child Psychology practical [3 marks AO2]

(ii) Explain two weaknesses in your Child Psychology Practical and how you could reduce them if you replicated the research. [4 marks AO2+AO3]

(c) Evaluate research in Child Psychology in terms of social sensitivity. [8 marks AO1+AO3]

(d) Assess the extent to which problems in child development are due to nurture rather than nature. [8 marks AO1+AO3]

(e) Assess the usefulness to society of cross-cultural research. [8 marks AO1+AO3]

(f) Assess the extent to which biological explanations of autism are more persuasive than other explanations. [16 marks AO1+AO3]

ABOUT THE AUTHOR

Jonathan Rowe is a teacher of Religious Studies, Psychology and Sociology at Spalding Grammar School and he creates and maintains **www.psychologywizard.net** and the **www.philosophydungeon.weebly.com** site for Edexcel A-Level Religious Studies. He has worked as an examiner for various Exam Boards but is not affiliated with Edexcel. This series of books grew out of the resources he created for his students. Jonathan also writes novels and creates resources for his hobby of fantasy wargaming. He likes warm beer and smooth jazz.

Printed in Great Britain
by Amazon

16546949R00066